DAY SPA
RESOURCE GUIDE

ALL THE GOOD HONEY IS IN HERE, & WHERE TO FIND IT

I dedicate this book to my mentors before me.

Those who encouraged me to never give up

and for writing this book. (thanks sis)

Copyrighted;ISBN: 9798811300730

ISBN: 9798854294683
ISBN: 9798811300730
ISBN: 9798705279401
ISBN: 9798705279401
ISBN: 9798655124288
ISBN: 9798705410989
ISBN-13: 978-1696073332
ISBN-10: 1696073332
ISBN-13: 978-1074641740
ISBN-10: 1074641744
ASIN: B07YDZK944

Special acknowledgments:

Contributing Editor Louisa Peck

Personal Story Contributors;

Michelle Larson, Tina Cardenas, Jill Zimmer, Shane Lowe, Fauzia Morgan.

Safety Standards, Washington State code; 3 Ch. WAC 308-20-110

Texas Texas Cosmetology Sanitation Laws 83.100.

Harvard Health Publishing, Dr. Gilchrest. Published October 2018

JESSECA M SMITH

How did I get started?

My experience in skincare dates back to 1992, when I worked as a cosmetics consultant and makeup artist for a major beauty retailer then later freelanced. After that, I had the opportunity to work with a natural -cosmetic chemist and co-create products for a natural beauty product line that sold in over 3,000 stores nationwide such as Nordstrom, Whole Foods, Wild Oats and Anthropologie. My goals gradually shifted from strictly wholesaling products to opening a Day Spa & Boutique — a concept that came to fruition in Dallas, Texas called Avocado Tree, eventually called Apothecurious Fresh Spa & Boutique.

Approached by many large box stores to buy out our concept, we eventually sold the business in 2008. Since then, I've had additional experience as a Body Care Manufacturer and Spa & Boutique Owner before eventually becoming an NIC board Licensed Esthetician. Operating first in Dallas as the Avocado Tree and later in Seattle, called Fresh Face Seattle. My spas were repeatedly written up by the press in glowing reviews and even voted *"Best Facial in Town."* It was an amazing experience. During this time, I discovered my love for mentoring and apprenticing budding Estheticians. Through this process and the culmination of my years in this business, I've grown to understand the importance of possessing a strong knowledge of ingredients, including their imperative freshness and effectiveness on our skin.

Now I bring my years of experience and love for the business to one guest (and apprentice) at a time and students in a classroom setting and finally, by sharing my knowledge and education with you. Enjoy! *Jesseca.*

PUBLISHED

Seattle Magazine 2009; Seattle Magazine 2008; NW Source 2008; American Spa 2008; Lucky Magazine consecutive months 2003-2006; Texas Monthly 2005; Dallas Observer 2004-2006; Paper City 2003-06; VAIN 2006; Modern Luxury 2005; The Olympian 2001; Wimberley View 2014; Hays County Press 2015; The Society Diaries 2016; San Antonio Woman February 2016; San Antonio Woman November/December issue 2016; SKIN INC 2021; Hill Country Chronicles December 2022; Voyage Austin December 2022, Welcome to Wimberley 2023: Canva Rebel Austin 2023: Best of Wimberley 2023: Best of Wimberley 2024: SkinInc 2024: SanAntonio Woman 2024.

BLOG, WORK & TRAININGS

BLOG available on MISSION Day Spa APP, missiondayspa.com, jessecamsmith.com webpage, Day Spa Resource Guide APP.

Find my CE courses available to the public at jessecamsmith.com

<u>Trainings;</u> Reiki Training Level I, II & Master 2001 & 2002
Member Permanent Cosmetics Society, 3D Brow Restoration Certified, Certified Cryoclear Specialist, Master Esthetics Junior-
Educator, Master Educator 2020
Oncology Esthetics Training, Cidesco 15 hours 2022
Oncology Esthetics Training, Oncology Training International 30 hours 2022

Advanced Esthetics Training continued education
years;2005,2006,2007,2008,2010,2012,2015,2016,2017,2018, 2021, 2022, 2024
Blood Born For Body Art Certificate
Permanent Cosmetics Operator license
Esthetician Operator license, Licensed Esthetics Educator, Licensed Continuing Education Provider
Salon Shop
Owner and CEO JMSE Management LLC, MISSION Day Spa
<u>Businesses,</u>
Joint ventures: Avocado Tree ©, Apothecurious ©, Spa Upstairs
Business's solely established; Fresh Face Seattle,
Jesseca M Smith Esthetics©, JMSE ELITE ©.

V

AN IDEA FOR NEW ESTHETI-CIANS

"Lots of honey in here!"

YOU MAY CHOOSE TO HOST ART PARTIES AND HAVE VENDORS

VI

INTRODUCTION

You've graduated as a licensed Esthetician, Cosmetologist,
Advanced Esthetician, Master Esthetician, or are an ARNP,
Dermatologist, LPN or Nurse Practitioner and are ready for a fresh
start in the Esthetics or Medical-
Aesthetics field.

NOW WHAT?

This is a comprehensive guide, drawing together all I've learned
from my many years in the spa field to help you get started.
Whether you want to start your own day spa with many employees
or run your own business independently, you probably have many
questions. This book is a resource to answer those questions and
provide an outline to guide you along your way. This is a template
I've used in my day spas I had in the past. It served as a tool I could
refer to my employees and managers alike for guidance and consis-
tence. I hope you find it useful. Utilize the fresh-mask selection
provided and most of all, have fun!

CONTENTS

THE SPA MANUAL

You may choose to use this portion of the book as a tool for your own Spa's Training and Protocol.

You may provide additional intake forms and may have them computer generated on digital templates. However, remember client confidentiality. Don't leave the files out in a public area and keep files locked away safe. Be sure information can't be shared or stolen and don't ever talk about clients who are visiting or have visited, especially in a medical setting because of privacy acts and HIPPA.

You can add additional policy and procedures to your manual as you choose, in addition to contractor forms. You can find contractor forms pre-made on Rocket Lawyer ™ for a fee with legal jargon appropriate to your states laws and rules.

Disclaimer: The views and opinions expressed by the author;

Jesseca M Smith do not necessarily reflect the official policy or position of any other entity, state board, legal or other; rather, simply are her culminated opinions after years of experience that have come together in this book to be in the most helpful way possible.

Section 1. The Spa Manual

A thorough intake form is priceless

<u>Client Intake Instructions</u>

1. If they are a new client, provide them with a "new client intake form" and ask them to fill it out completely.

2. Review the intake form. Be sure all questions are answered.

3. Highlight if they have mentioned any allergies, and continue the allergy list on the back of the page in the allergies and notes section. Be sure this is also highlighted.

4. Check to see that the client has signed the intake form, and understands your policies.

5. Each client should receive a skin analysis. This should be performed with each and every service.

6. Tell your client their skin type.

7. Ask what it is they expect while receiving the facial, and discuss any questions or concerns.

8. Remember, YOU are the expert. Give them <u>what they never knew they wanted</u>! Basically go above and beyond. Remember, you're in the service industry after all.

MY GORGEOUS SISTER AND INSPIRATION FOR WRITING THIS BOOK!

Industry leader spotlight Michelle Larson. Michelle was inspired to become a salon owner after many years moving up in the ranks as long time booth renter. She owns a successful salon in her hometown of Olympia, WA and has a loyal following. In the industry since 1996, Michelle apprentices budding cosmo's and gives back to the community often.

Find her personal story at the back of the book.

I _________________________________agree to have eyelash extensions applied to my natural eyelashes and/or removed and retouched. By signing this agreement, I consent to the placement and/or removal of the eyelash extensions by the certified eyelash extension professional.

_______ I understand that in rare occasions there are risks associated with having artificial eyelashes and eyelash extensions applied to or removed from my natural eyelashes. I further understand that in rare cases as part of the procedure eye irritation and discomfort could occur. I agree that if I experience any of these conditions with my lashes that I will contact the certified eyelash extension professional that performed this procedure and it may be beneficial to have the eyelashes removed.

_______ I understand and agree to the after-care instructions provided by the certified eyelash extension professional for the use and care of my eyelash extensions. I realize and accept the consequences of failure to adhere to these instructions may cause the eyelash extensions to fall out and/or decrease the time the lashes will last.

_______ I understand and consent to having my eyes closed and covered for the duration of approximately 60-120 minute procedure. Times may vary depending on the type and number of eyelashes applied.

_______ I am informing the certified eyelash extension professional of the following conditions by marking with a check:

- ☐ Current use of contact lenses which I may be asked to remove during the procedure
- ☐ Current use of anything such as oil-containing sunscreen or moisturizers around the eyes
- ☐ Current use of eye drops of any kind, prescription or over-the-counter
- ☐ Current allergies or sensitivities
- ☐ History of recurrent eye or tear duct infections
- ☐ History of dry eyes or Sjorgen's Syndrome
- ☐ Recent history of Chemotherapy
- ☐ Other medical conditions which would prohibit or compromise placement and retention of eyelash extensions
- ☐

_______ I agree to the following eyelash extension follow-up and maintenance instructions:

- ☐ No waterproof mascara
- ☐ No oil based products around the eye area
- ☐ No water can come in contact with the eye area for 24 hours after the application
- ☐ No tinting or perming of eyelash extensions
- ☐ No pulling or rubbing of the eyelash extensions
- ☐ Should any kind of eye drops be necessary extra care should be taken to prevent moisture from coming into contact with the eyelash extensions

This agreement will remain in effect for this procedure and all future follow-ups conducted by the certified eyelash extension professional. I read English and understand that this consent agreement is legal and binding. I have read and fully understand all information in this agreement. I am over 18 years of age and consent to the agreement and to the eyelash extension application procedure.

CLIENT NAME:

____

CLENT SIGNATURE:

____

EMAIL: _____________________
PHONE: _____________________
DATE: _____________________

TECH NAME:

____

TECH SIGNATURE:

____

EMAIL: _____________________
PHONE: _____________________
DATE: _____________________

SAMPLE EYELASH EXTENSION CONSENT FORM

Skin Care History

Name: ____ Date: _____________

Address: ____

City: _____________________________ State: ___________ Zip: __________

Email Address: ____

Cell Phone: _______________________ Date of Birth: _________________

Emergency Contact: ___________________________ Phone: ____________

Are you pregnant: Yes ❑ No ❑   If yes, how far along: ________________________

Do you have any of the following health conditions:

❑ AIDS/HIV   ❑ Heart Problems   ❑ Lupus
❑ Cancer   ❑ Hepatitis   ❑ Recent Surgeries
❑ Diabetes   ❑ High/Low Blood Pressure   ❑ Strokes

Please list any other health conditions not listed above: ________________________

____

Are you currently using any of the following?

❑ Retin A/Renova   ❑ Hydroquinone
❑ Glycolic Acid/Alpha Hydroxy Acid ❑ Hormone Replacement Therapy
❑ Accutane   ❑ Birth Control Pills
❑ Topical Vitamin C   ❑ Sunscreen/Sun Block

If yes, please list the names of any prescription medication(s): ________________________

____

Are you using or have ever used any medications for acne? ❑ Yes   ❑ No
If yes, how long has it been since you last used acne medication?________________________

Do you suffer from Cold Sores? ❑ Yes   ❑ No If yes, do you take medication? ❑ Yes ❑ No
Do you smoke?   ❑ Yes ❑ No
Do you tan?   ❑ Yes ❑ No
Have you had facials before?   ❑ Yes ❑ No
Have you had electrolysis, laser hair removal, or waxing in the last week? ❑ Yes   ❑ No

What skin care products are you currently using? ________________________

____

14

Wrap Client Intake and Release Form

Client Name: _______________________ Phone (C): _____________ (W): _____________
Address: _______________________ City: __________ State: ______ Zip Code: ______
E-Mail: _______________________ Referred By: _______________________
Date Of Birth: ____/____/____
Occupation: _______________ Exercise Level: _______________________
Emergency Contact: _____________ Relationship To Client: ___________ Phone: ______

Have you ever used an Infrared Sauna or Body Wrap: Circle Yes or No

Reason for Visit: Motivation, expectations:

____

Number of Wraps Purchased: _____________ Date of Initial Wrap: _____________

Contra-Indications for Infrared Body Wraps

☐ Cardiac Conditions
☐ Lupus Erythematosus
☐ Adrenal suppression
☐ Multiple Sclerosis
☐ Metal Pins or Rods
☐ Artificial Joints
☐ Implanted Silicone
☐ Varicose Veins
☐ Heavy Menstruation
☐ Acute Joint Injury 1st 48 Hours
☐ Implanted Pacemaker
☐ Pregnancy

☐ Constricted Coronary Blood Vessels
☐ High & Low Blood Pressure
☐ Enclosed Infections (Dental, Joint)
☐ Hemophilia
☐ Overactive Thyroid Gland
☐ Diabetes Requiring Insulin
☐ Kidney Malfunctions
☐ Open Wounds
☐ Skin Diseases
☐ Contact Allergies
☐ Fever
☐ Severe General Infection

Other/ Please Describe: ____

Consult your doctor before receiving an Infrared Body Wrap treatment if you have received treatment for any of the above listed conditions in the highlighted area. You can not receive the treatment if you suffer from any of the remaining conditions described above. If you have a history of any other medical condition or you are taking prescription drugs, you should consult your physician before using the Formostar Infrared Body Wrap.

Doctors Name: _______________________ Telephone: _______________________
Doctors Approval : Written ( ) Verbal ( )

I have been fully informed and understand the use of the Formostar Encore Body Wrap System and accept personal responsibility for my treatments. I understand that Agave Massage, LLC and its staff are not liable for any injury to person caused in any way by the use of its services or premises. I am aware that the results achieved by this treatment may vary from person to person, and I acknowledge that no promises or guarantees have been made to me as to the results of this treatment.

Client Signature: _______________________ Date: _______________________

* You are advised to use the restroom prior to the treatment.

Sample General Body Wrap Intake Form

Suggested Basic Facial Room Equipment
Table
Towel warmer
Mag lamp
Back Bar
Towels
Sheets
Gowns for guests

Suggested Advanced Facial Room Equipment
Contoured Table
Towel warmer
Mag lamp with steamer and high frequency
My Skin Buddy
Back Bar
Towels
Sheets
Gowns for guests

Suggested Elite Facial Room Equipment
Hydraulic Table
Towel warmer with ozone
8 in 1 machine
Back Bar
LED
My Skin Buddy
Microcurrent
Microdermabrasion
Towels
Sheets
Gowns for guests

Suggested Medical Facial Room Equipment
Hydraulic Table
Towel warmer with ozone
8 in 1 machine
Back Bar
LED
My Skin Buddy
Microcurrent
Microdermabrasion
Hydrafacial Machine
Microneedling Pen
Dermaplane Scalpels
Towels
Sheets
Gowns for guests
Refrigerator for injectables

ROOM SET UP

Section 1a. Room Set up and Clean up

<u>*AM shift*</u>

1. Make sure each room is ready for the guests according to the treatment type.
2. Be sure all implements, bowls and brushes are clean and ready to be used.
3. Light all candles and heat the rooms accordingly and in a timely manner.
4. Be sure you have all the necessary masks and supplies from the dispensary according to the treatment.
5. Check to make sure if all equipment is clean, ready to use, and working.

<u>*After each appointment*</u>

1. Treatment table is ready for next guest.
2. Floor is clean and sanitary, and a fresh towel is down.
3. Candles are lit and room is warm.
4. Masks and other supplies appropriate for the next treatment are in the room.

<u>*Closing*</u>

1. Treatment table is ready for the next day.

2. Floor is cleaned/mopped and sanitized.

3. Your set-up should be clean, sanitized and ready for the next day.

4. Equipment should be clean and ready for the next day

Note: ***Do not leave without cleaning up the treatment rooms and getting them ready for the next day's services. The inspector may be waiting for you when you arrive the next day! Be ready!***

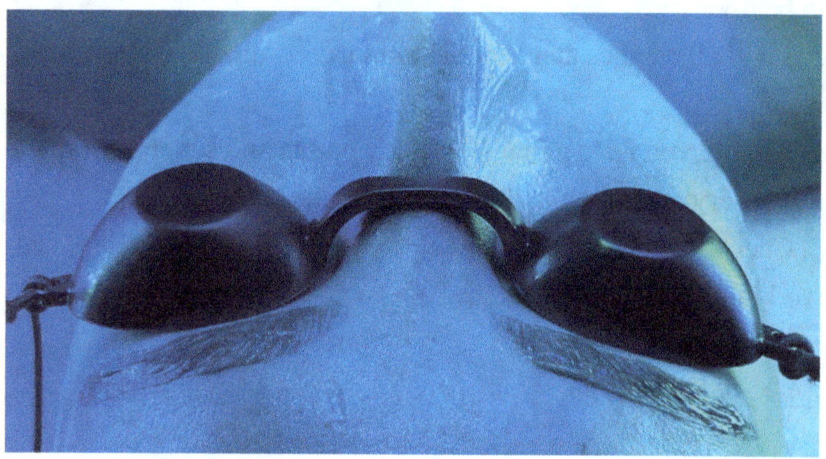

LED IS COMMONLY USED
TO ENHANCE FACIAL TREATMENTS-
DIFFERENT COLOR LED LIGHT PENETRATES THE SKIN AT DIFFERENT DEPTHS, THEREBY PROVIDING DIFFERENT RESULTS BASED ON THE COLOR LIGHT BEING EMITTED.
Know your colors!
LED light has been found to produce results with regular use over a period of time, usually 8-12 weeks. This is a non-invasive treatment with virtually no downtime, making it an upgrade to your clients.

Each LED light color penetrates the skin differently.
Blue light is an antibacterial agent.
Red light is an anti-inflammatory. Near-infrared light stimulates cell activity and increases production of collagen and elastin.
Yellow light helps the lymph system to detoxify your body.
Green light decreases melanin production and reduces redness.

<u>*The Appointment*</u>

1. Get to your appointment on time. Ten minutes early is on time.
2. Thank your client warmly and *at once* for coming.
3. Realize the first few minutes of an appointment are crucial, be sure to get things off to a great start.
4. Look and act professional before, during and after your appointment.
5. Be sure to mention your client's name at least four times during the appointment, to ensure your full attention is theirs.
6. Be sure to emphasize how the products you are using will benefit their skin care needs.
7. Be sure to thank your client after the service is over, and invite them to come back and see you again! Write them a thank you note and have it mailed by the week's end.

* Captivate your client with the individuality your company's concept offers and attention to detail with not only its products, but also the services. You are the ultimate representation of your company and all it has to offer. Be sure to note you're recommended products and the ingredients. Follow up with a client and invite them back. *Always send a thank you note. And take good notes on the client file.* Speak from your heart and genuinely be yourself.

* We are glad to have you as a part of our team!

DRESS CODE

1. No jeans.

2. Comfortable shoes are acceptable. They should not have an excessively worn look or be dirty.

3. Hair should be pulled away from the face <u>*at all times*</u>.

4. Estheticians should never wear scented deodorant, perfumes or hair products.

5. You must not smell of vape, cigarette smoke (or any kind of smoke) or alcohol *ever*.

6. A uniform, apron or smock may be provided. If so, it must be worn while on the clock and for your shift. Smocks or aprons may be determined by your employer.

7. You are responsible for the cleanliness of your attire, including your scrubs. If your uniform is dirty, take it home and wash it. (unscented detergent)

8. Fingernails must be clean, short and well manicured without polish.

9. Minimal makeup with a clean and fresh look.

TREATMENTS

Section 1c. Treatments and Procedures

Express or Mini Facial (30 minutes)

Room Set Up and Supplies:

6 steamed towels

Pull customized masks after skin evaluation

Top sheet

Bottom sheet

1-2 candles (for room ambience/optional)

Pillow or knee bolster for under the legs

Neck roll optional

Client stays dressed

Large towel to drape over client

Blanket for client comfort

Steps:

1. Drape client's clothes and hair with large towel over body, hand towel for hair.

2. Cleanse with appropriate cleanser twice.

3. Spray toner (optional) and apply eye pads at this time.

4. Apply lip conditioning treatment and aromatherapeutic treatment to nose and lips if available.

5. Perform skin analysis.

6. Steam the skin with towels or steamer max 10 minutes.

7. Exfoliate the skin while steaming with appropriate exfoliant or use MYSKINBUDDY © .

8. Tone the skin.

9. Apply appropriate toner and moisturizer.

10. Use high frequency to penetrate products if necessary or appropriate.

Be sure to invite the client back. Max time is 30 minutes. This is a great lunch time facial.

Notes:

____

____

____

____

____

____

____

____

____

____

*Clean your steamer every week with 1 cap white vinegar and distilled water.

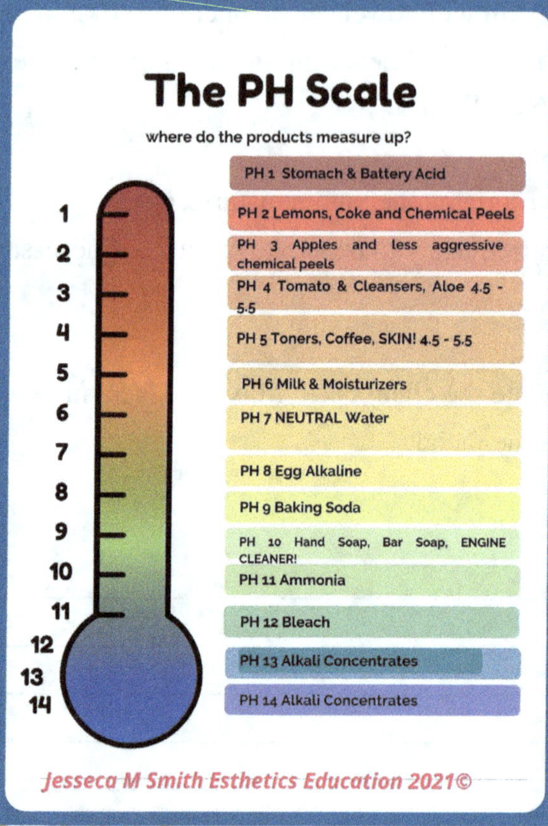

CHOOSE PRODUCTS BASED ON SKIN TYPE AND NEEDS- BUT ALWAYS BE AWARE OF THE PH FACTOR. WHAT ARE YOUR CLIENTS REALLY USING? COMPARE TO THE PH SCALE TO EDUCATE THEM. ***DR BRONNERS SOAP MAY BE NATURAL BUT IS AS ALKALINE AS ENGINE CLEANER***.

Fresh European-Style Facial (70+ minutes)

Room Set Up and Supplies:

Down comforter (or alternative down) Knee pillow

Top and bottom sheets

Pull appropriate masks after skin evaluation

Foot scrub optional

Steps:

1. Cleanse your guest's skin with appropriate cleanser twice.

2. Remove cleanser and tone with optional toner or witch hazel.

3. Apply cool eye pads.

4. Apply an exfoliant or *Fresh Papaya Enzyme Mask (see Recipes section)* and leave on for 10 minutes.

5. Massage each hand for 5 minutes while masking, then after, wrap each hand with a fresh warm towel.

6. Use your massage method #1 with massage lotion infused with drops of essential oil for aromatherapy (optional). REMEMBER! Massage is your signature!!! Refer to the app for proper massage techniques under "facialing".

7. Cleanse the skin again.

8. Tone the skin.

9. Apply appropriate mask or *Fresh Cucumber Mask* (see Recipes section) leave on for 10 minutes.

10. Gently scrub the feet while client's skin is masking and remove the scrub with warm steamy towels.

11. Apply steamed towels one at a time for maximum 3 minutes each.

12. Remove the mask with the last towel, gently.

13. Spray your mist or toner if necessary.

14. Apply blemish formula to areas that may be affected by blemishes.

15. Apply appropriate facial serum for mature skin types.

16. Apply appropriate moisturizer to face and neck.

17. Use high-frequency to penetrate products into the skin (optional)

18. Advise client that treatment is over and begin to pull products to recommend them. Do not forget to schedule their next appoint-

Notes:

____

____

____

____

Gentlemen's Facial (60 minutes)

Room Set Up and Supplies:

Steamer with ozone

3 steamed towels

Pull customized masks after skin evaluation

Top sheet

Bottom sheet and knee bolster

Neck roll or pillow Robe

Candles

Steps:

1. Cleanse with appropriate cleanser twice.

2. Tone the skin with toner or witch hazel.

3. Apply lip balm and aromatherapy if available.

4. Steam with ozone on for 10 minutes.

5. Scrub the skin with appropriate exfoliant or *Fresh Papaya Enzyme Mask* 5 minutes.

6. Remove the exfoliate with clean sponges and warm water.

7. Use massage technique #1 apply massage lotion (infused with three drops of eucalyptus essential oil for aromatherapy, optional) for 10 minutes.

8. Gently remove with cleanser appropriate to skin type.

9. Apply appropriate mask or Organic Banana Mask (available in recipes section).

10. Massage the hands and arms while masking, 5 minutes each.

11. Apply fresh eye pads, generally cotton rounds wet with distilled water.

12. Remove the mask with warm steamy towels.

13. Spritz the skin with toner or witch hazel (optional).

14. Apply a light layer of skin appropriate serum followed by moisturizer.

15. Advise guest that treatment is finished and pull products to recommend. Don't forget to schedule his next appointment.

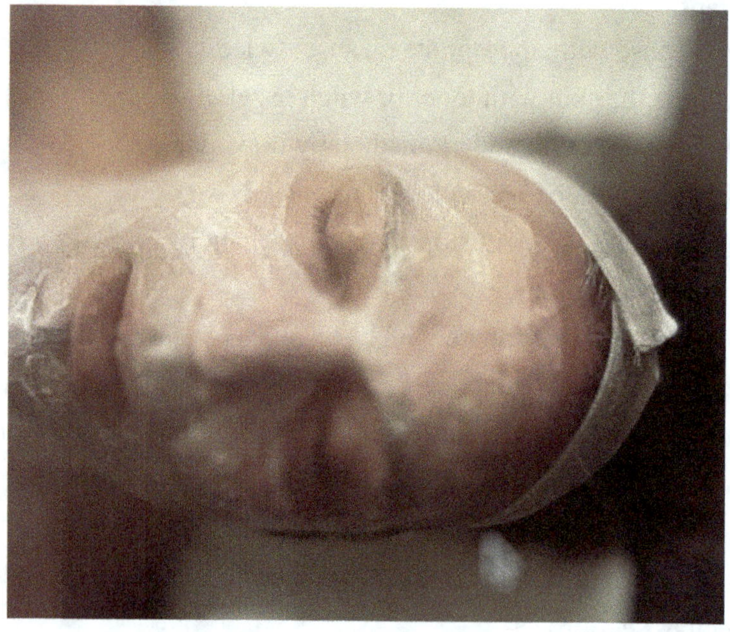

Gentlemen's Facial Model

Micro-dermabrasion Treatment (60 minutes)

Room Set Up and Supplies:

Microdermabrasion machine

Mag lamp

Cool towels

Facial cap if using crystals

Goggles (if needed)

Face mask for Esthetician (if needed)

Eye pads

Recovery mask

Vinyl gloves

Top sheet

Candles

Robe

Steps:

1. Cleanse the skin with appropriate cleanser.

2. Tone the skin.

3. Dry the skin with lint-free cotton pads.

4. Protect the eyes with barely damp eye pads.

5. Adjust the Microderm machine pressure for client's needs and desired outcome.

6. Perform Microdermabrasion treatment for three passes all over the client's face, neck, décolleté and backs of hands.

7. Remove the remaining crystals from the skin the cleansing with appropriate cleanser.

8. Spritz facial mist or toner to soothe.

9. Apply cooling recovery mask or *Fresh Cucumber Mask* or *Fresh Avocado Mask*, over appropriate serum.

10. Massage hands while masking 5-10 minutes.

11. Remove mask with cool/damp towels.

12. Tone with soothing rosewater toner or toner of choice.

13. Apply thin layer of Vitamin C serum, followed by moisturizer.

14. Give client instructions on at home care.

15. *Remember NO SUN for 24 hours! No active at home facial care.*

Fresh Ingredients for Fresh Masks

Clinical Style-Facial (60 minutes)

Note: the clinical facial is for clients with problematic skin types such as acne, cuprous, rosacea, papules and pustules, comedones, millia and seborrhea. Each service may be modified to meet each persons specific skin care need.

Room Set Up and Supplies:
3-6 steamy towels
Access to steamer with ozone
Mag lamp and woods lamp
Extractor kit
Pull customized masks after skin evaluation
Vinyl gloves
Steps:

1. Cleanse twice.
2. Tone.
3. Apply eye pads.
4. Look at client's skin under mag lamp.
5. Let client know what their skin type is, what you see and recommend. Ask what products they are using and what results they anticipate from receiving this facial (basically, what they plan to do to continue the results and satisfaction).
6. Cleanse again.

7. Steam with ozone for 5 minutes.

8. Apply an enzyme mask while steaming or you may choose a facial peel such as the *Fresh Papaya Enzyme Mask (see Recipes section)*, for additional 5 minutes, if skin type allows.

9. Apply just desincrustation solution if skin type allows, and you are unable to give an enzyme mask.

10. Remove steam and mask with cool sponges and water.

11. Apply massage oil and massage #1 with each movement totaling 5 minutes.

12. Remove with cleanser and steamy towel.

13. Perform extractions if needed at this time.

14. Apply a clay mask according to skin type add essential oils that are appropriate for the desired results, maximum 10 minutes.

15. Massage hands while masking. After, wrap hands with fresh towels.

16. Remove with steamy towels.

17. Apply blemish stick compressions to calm down areas. Apply blemish treatment or aloe compresses to inflamed areas.

18. Tone the skin.

19. Apply appropriate serum or moisturizer appropriate to skin type. Finish by using the high-frequency machine be sure to check for contraindications for using this machine such as heart conditions or heart monitor, etc.

20. Provide a skin profile for your guest to take home.

21. Pull the recommended products and schedule follow-up treatments and provide at home skincare regimen. Remember, you are the expert.

Professional Facial Peel or Glycolic Peel (45 minutes)

Room set up and Supplies:
Glycolic peel max 33% (or approved by state) unless approved by Doctor/Dermatologist
Baking soda water solution ice cold, unless peel is self neutralizing (This is 1 teaspoon to 1/2 cup water)
Cotton pads at least 10
Small fan
Isopropyl Alcohol
Top sheet
Head wrap
Knee bolster for comfort
Robe to protect clothing
Vinyl gloves

Steps:

1. Cleanse the skin thoroughly *twice*.
2. Be sure to rinse the skin very well.
3. Tone the skin.
4. Protect the eyes and nose with aromatherapeutic oil.
5. Apply lip balm to the lips.
6. Using a damp cotton round, apply isopropyl alcohol to remove any remaining dirt and oil from the skin... Avoiding mucous membrane areas.
7. Begin applying Peel Glycolic Gel 33% (higher if you are a Master Esthetician in a medical setting), Beta, Alpha Hydroxy or other peel to the forehead. Work briskly forehead to chin.

8. Do not rub it in.

9. Fan the client for comfort.

10. Leave application on for a minimum of 3 minutes. No more than twelve. Watch for redness, check for heat. **Remove immediately if too irritated.**

11. Remove solution with cold baking soda water to neutralize (unless self-neutralizing). Keep rinsing until client reports no more tingling.

12. Only use a spray toner at this time.

13. Apply appropriate skin soothing facial mask such as the *Fresh Cucumber Mask* or *Soothing Oat Mask (see Recipes section).*

14. Leave the soothing mask on max 10 minutes while massaging the hands.

15. Remove the mask with cool moist towels DO NOT RUB and tone again.

16. Apply appropriate moisturizer and be sure to instruct the client for proper skin maintenance and this includes *no sun* for at least 72 hours.

Notes:

____

____

____

____

Notes:

____

____

____

____

Body Wrap or Body Scrub (60 minutes)

Room Set Up and Supplies:

Sugar and oil body scrub with client's chosen essential oils for aromatherapy or enough

clay mask to cover the entire body, usually one small mixing cupful.

Large body brush

Plastic sheeting

2 top sheets lying sideways

8 steamy towels

2 dry sponges

Small room heater for comfort

Extra blanket for comfort

Wet room

Lay 2 flat sheets sideways on the table.

Leave the plastic sheet on top of the two sheets.

Roll one large towel for the neck.

Include two other large towels for body draping. Instruct the client to use

one to drape the bust, and the other to drape the waist.

Steps:

1. Instruct your client to remove all clothing and to use the two large towels to dry, then have client get on the table still sitting up.

2. Begin service by using the dry sponges to "dry-brush the skin" using upwards strokes towards heart.

3. Apply the mask or body scrub to their back, then have them lay down. *Work quickly.*

4. Have client bend the knees so you can reach under each leg, then lay flat.

5. Grab the plastic sheet around their body snugly, but comfortably.

6. Wrap the sheets lying sideways around the plastic sheet to insulate.

7. Turn a room heater on for comfort.

8. Massage the client's temples with aromatherapy for 10 minutes.

9. Leave the room and clean your water bowl if no sink in room; *be sure to not leave the client for more than 3 minutes* unless they have a way to alert you (for example, a bell) in case they have an emergency or immediate need.

10. Upon return, check on your client to be sure they aren't overheating. Begin removing the blankets and sheets.

11. Apply warm, damp towels over body, section by section, and wipe to remove the mask or scrub. Please note, for your client's comfort, remove the scrub after the skin has been thoroughly *body polished.*

12. Wipe the floor and lay down a fresh towel for client to step on.

13. *Invite your client back for additional services.*

Note: You may integrate other modalities into this style of facial. For instance, Microcurrent, Ultrasonic, LED, Paraffin Facial Mask, An Advanced Peel or excuse the room for the Doctor to return for an injection treatment and end the service with a real bang! Whatever the case, all these facials listed in this book are just basic protocols and can easily be built into upgradeable services.

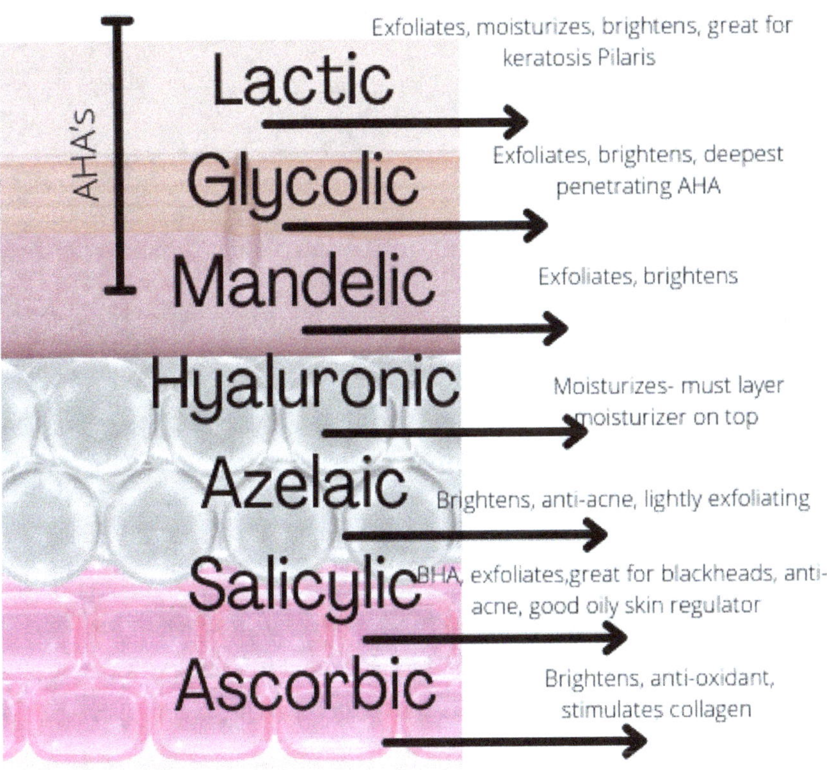

KNOW YOUR PEELS AND WHAT THEY DO

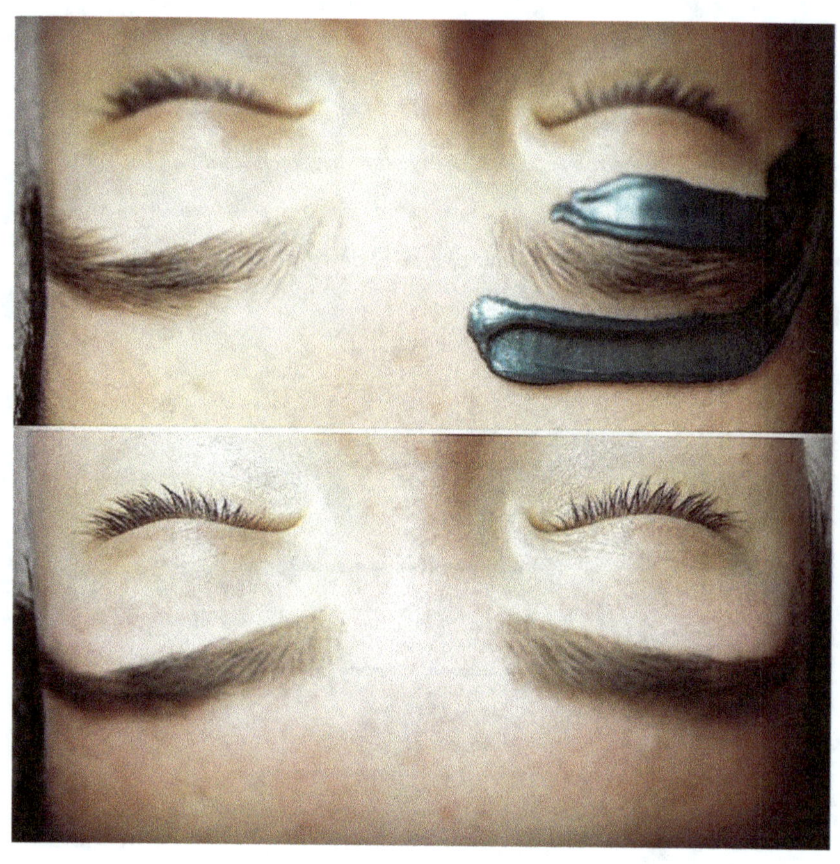

Eye brow Wax Model

Note: It is still advisable to perform scrubs and body wraps in a facility that provides a shower but, if you don't have a shower and you are using products that include clay masks, butters, creams or scrubs, the key is to be sure the guest is completely free of these products after the treatment is over. Be sure to check toes, behind elbows, etc. This will add to your level of profession-alism and care.

38

Waxing, sugaring and hair removal of *all* kinds should be done in a completely separate room (in my opinion) unless you are a single practitioner and/or only doing facial waxing. It's a very sticky and messy treatment. You can double your earning potential if you have the means to take on the additional overhead at first. Keep the *sticky* away from the spa space. You'll be so happy you did this. These rooms *must* be kept very clean with easy to sanitize, non-porous surfaces. In addition, if you are in a setting that also offers Microblading or are an Esthetician and also a Permanent Cosmetics or Tattoo Artist, you may use the waxing room for these purposes. Tattoo Artists cannot have any linens, towels, blankets or anything that blood borne pathogens can adhere to, and so a waxing room *doubling* as a tattoo room often works. Be sure to double-check with your State to be sure there isn't any law or code prohibiting this.

If you wish to offer spray tans, they require ventilation and I would also recommend a wet room. *For Medical Spas, be sure the spa is run and owned by a collaborating physician or medical doctor. Check with your laws. If you need a cp, <u>look up Aesthetic Medical Partners, Collaborating Docs or Doctors for providers.</u>

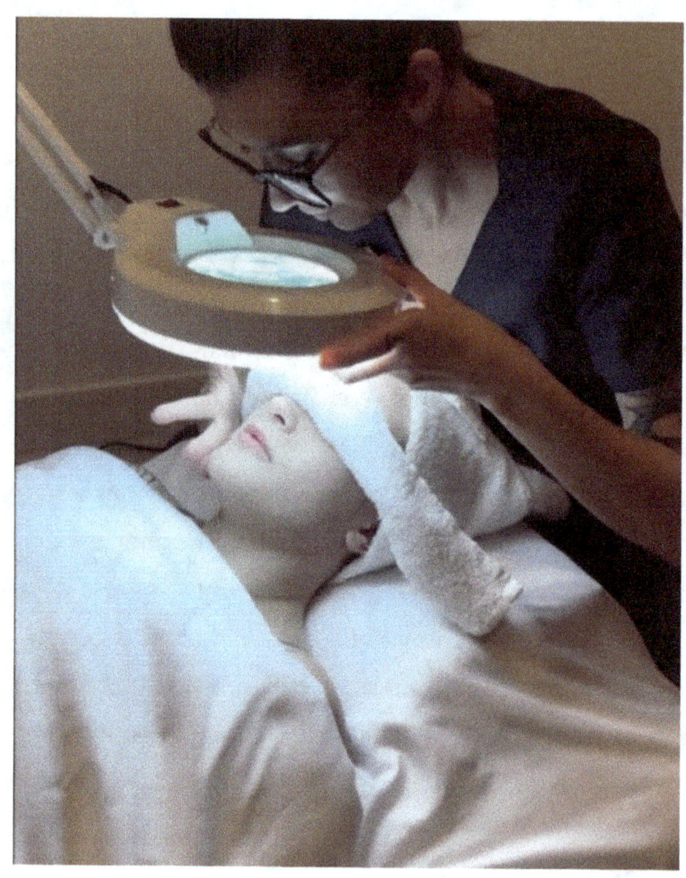

What is a collaborating physician??

The physician will be your medical director so they will meet all of your state's requirements as a medical director. The physician has to be listed as the owner of the PC (professional corporation) and you will be the MSO holder which manages everything non medical.

How to Handle a Dissatisfied Client

This may happen more than once, and definitely to all of us at one time or another. How do we handle a stressful situation? How do we satisfy the dissatisfied client? It really depends on the situation.

Was it an allergic reaction? If severe, dial 911. If not, you can suggest an antihistamine. Generally, if a reaction is occurring as a treatment is being performed, use the baking soda solution (1 teaspoon to 1/2 cup water) to neutralize the skin. You may also soothe the skin with cucumber and oatmeal, if appropriate. Send the client home with a recommendation to call their doctor, especially if the reaction worsens. Also recommend they take an antihistamine and be sure to follow up. Suggest the client notify their doctor of *all* allergic reactions.

Was the client not satisfied with the treatment they received? Assess the situation. Ask questions. Reassure that you are here for them. Ask for feedback; how could you have provided the type of service they really anticipated? This information is for you but always refer to their intake form for clarity.

You must trust your judgment in the moment since they are rarely the same. When a client is dissatisfied, whether it is your fault or not, they must be handled cautiously. Try, by all means, to remedy the situation. Offer a complementary service or discount on product. If all else fails, refer them to the lead Esthetician or Manager.

If they aren't immediately available, direct the client to fill out a comment card and that they will be contacted shortly. Still remember to thank them for being your guest, and that you appreciate their patronage.

If in a Spa setting, and when in doubt, *always* refer guests to the Spa Manager. Have them use their expertise in customer service to remedy the situation. If you are a sole practitioner, speak from your heart and be genuine. Imagine yourself in their shoes.

Notes:

____

____

____

____

____

____

____

____

____

____

____

SKIN TYPES

Section 1d. Recognizing Skin Types

Knowing the Fitzpatrick scale and skin typing is key

CLASSIFICATION MEASURE FOR PHOTO AGEING

GLOGAU

the wrinkle scale

Notes:

____

____

____

____

1. **Dehydration.** Any skin type may suffer from dehydration. It is more of a condition rather than a real skin type or problem. A dehydrated skin type lacks water, has a course texture and loss of firmness. Dehydrated skin can be caused from sun, excessive harsh drying agents, and lack of moisture.

2. **Comedogenic/Comedones.** Usually are caused by lack of exfoliation of dead, dry skin cells. The skin is usually oily, it but appears dry due to a lack of exfoliation; the oils are trapped in the layers below and cannot reach the surface to lubricate. Often a customer will be sold a moisturizer that adds to the oilfield, instead of a mask to pull out the impurities.

3. **Florid (pale) Skin**. Is an indication of a fine, translucent skin that is usually sensitive to strong products. The skin is tight and it should avoid cleansing grains, strong alcohol and extreme temperatures.

4. **Brown Spots**. A result of overproduction of melanin. Can be caused by hormonal imbalance, sun exposure or both. Can be small or large-Melasma, Chloasma, Freckles. Usually manifest after 40.

18 known rosacea triggers

- Sun exposure
- Hot weather
- Hot showers
- Intense workouts
- Humidity
- Indoor heat
- Hot drinks
- Marinated meat
- Some medications

- Stress
- Cold weather
- Strong wind
- Alcoholic beverages
- Spicy food
- Certain cosmetics
- Citrus
- Dairy
- Overheating

ⓘ Heads-up: your triggers are unique.
Not all of these triggers may apply to your specific rosacea.

ROSACEA TRIGGERS

"Higher concentrations of hydroquinone can cause white spots to develop on the skin," says Dr. Gilchrest. The medication may even cause a darkening of the skin in some cases. Your dermatologist might also recommend kojic acid or azelaic acid, which are other topical skin lightening agents, she says. Other treatments that are sometimes recommended for melasma include chemical peels,

Lasers! Chemical Peels! Micro-needling! Oh MY!

Even advanced Permanent Cosmetics Artists are combating hyper-pigmentation by using the superficial technique of micro-needling lighter pigments into the skins surface! Be sure you're aware of the Fitzpatrick scale, how the skin will handle these advanced treatments and the long-term outcomes. Studies have shown that hyper-pigmentation sometime's manifest simply from the heat of ones own cheeks. Be careful. Use your best judgment. Don't work outside your scope of practice. Be sure you take the "less is more" approach. Coach your client that *less is more*. I've always said this and have coined it as one of my own mottos:
"I do my best and forgive the rest". We are lucky to age, and most want to do it as gracefully as we can.

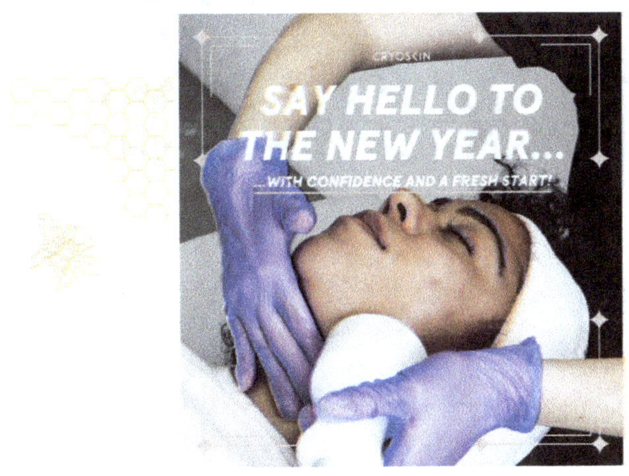

CAPTIVATE YOUR CLIENTS WITH
INNOVATIVE SERVICES

CREATE YOUR OWN RECIPES WITH WHAT
YOU KNOW FROM THE PH SCALE

RECIPES &...

Chocolate Mask: Soothing & moisturizing

Blend 2Tbsp Organic Local Honey, 1/4 cup distilled water or rose toner, 1 tsp castor oil, with one heaping Tbsp Local Organic Unsweetened Cocoa Powder and blend until creamy.

Milk brightening mask: Natural Lactic Peel

1/4 cup Organic Dried Milk
1 heaping tsp Organic Dried Lavender Petals (grind them in coffee grinder)
1 tsp Local Organic Honey.
1/4 cup Rose Toner.
Blend until creamy.

Soothing Oat Mask:

2 Tbsp Organic Oats. 2 Tbsp Rose Toner.
2 Tbsp Distilled Water. Make a paste.

Fresh Avocado Mask: Moisturizing & lightening

Blend until creamy, one peeled Organic Avocado with 2 Tbsp Local Organic Honey and 1tsp Organic, Sugar Free Yogurt.
Must make fresh. Will not keep.

PRIVATE LABEL SPA ESSENTIALS AT OUR FLAGSHIP SPA FOR
PRIVATE CONSULTATION ON HOW TO OWN YOUR OWN START
UP SPA

Fresh Papaya Enzyme Mask: Exfoliating & brightening

Remove pulp from small ripe papaya add 1/4 cup honey

add 2 tsp fresh lemon juice

add 2 tsp fresh lime juice add 1 tsp grape-seed oil

blend in blender until smooth.

Keep in refrigerator for 5 days. *Will become gelatinous.*

*Use as a quick pick - me - up enzyme peel. The mask lifts dead skin
and reveals fresh, bright happy skin.*

50

Fresh Cucumber Mask: Use after Microdermabrasion or Chemical Peels.

One Fresh Organic Cucumber sliced and peeled. If using entire cucumber at once, add 4x the remaining ingredients and keep refrigerated up to one week.
Add the following...

3 1-inch slices of cucumber.
2Tbsp Organic Oats.
1Tbsp Organic Local Honey (optional) 2 Tbsp Organic Rose Water or Toner Blend/Mix in blender until creamy.

Organic Banana Mask: Great for Mens Skin, soothing & brightening

One peeled organic banana. If using entire banana at once, add 4x the remaining ingredients and keep refrigerated up to one week.
Add the following...
2Tbsp Organic, Sugar Free Yogurt
2Tbsp Organic Local Honey Blend/Mix util creamy.

NOTE: *All fresh masks listed will not keep for more than 3-6 days in a refrigerator. Date each batch for freshness.*

In 2008, shortly after I moved to Seattle, I was published in this American Spa Magazine for hand mixing natural skincare and featuring it in my Esthetics practice. This particular article shared the Fresh Avocado Mask and its recipe. Now I share it with you!

FLOOR PLAN SAMPLES

Section 2. Floor plans

KEEP YOUR SUITE EASY TO CLEAN, SIMPLE AND FREE OF CLUT-
TER. YOU MAY CHOOSE TO USE LOCKERS OR ARMOIRES TO
STORE LINENS AND ESSENTIAL SUPPLIES.

Whether in a salon suite or a stand alone building, design your space with the intention of your clients comfort in mind. Think of color scheme… Think of where you will be storing your extra product. Where are they going to hang their coat, put their shoes… Are you going to provide a gown? Think about how   easily it'll be to clean all surfaces. Non slip floor?   Easily mopped ? All important decisions. A typical treatment room in a spa ranges from square feet 90 to 120 (10x12 room is 120 sq ft). If you plan to have machines like a laser in that room, it is essential to increase the size from 120 to 140 square feet. If you plan to do couples treatments, double that size plus ten feet.

Flow is everything. Design your own floorplans on Canva, SmartDraw, Room-Sketcher, Foyer, RoomPlanner or hire a professional architect/ designer. Have fun with this!

Section 3. Vendors & Suppliers

Purchase good equipment from reputable suppliers! I cannot stress this enough. Amazon seems great at first but are there equipment-warranties? Can you return if equipment is faulty? Are they trusted suppliers? Is the equipment worth while?

Skin Buddy
MDSpaShop
Oncology Spa Solutions
LCL Beauty
Universal Companies
Massage Warehouse
Salon Centric
Salon Services
M. Spa & Esthetics Supply
theSpaMart
Lost Artistry Lash
Meyerspa Medical Spa and Supply
Blaso Suppliers
Schedulista online scheduler
MDPHOTO app for medical photos
Mindbody
SQUARE
Gloss Genius
Lavishlash
Vinlash
Selfnamed Skincare

Hale & Hush haleandhush.com **for professionals ONLY**

Elaa Skincare elaaskincare.com

Solavedi Organics solavediorganics.com

Kindred Skincare www.kindredskincareco.com

Starflower Essentials www.starflower.com

Circadia circadia.com

Tata Harper Skincare www.have2have.it/tataharper

ELTA www.eltamd.com

SkinCeuticals www.skinceuticals.com

Skin Medica www.skinmedica.com

Obagi www.obagi.com

Avène www.aveneusa.com

PCA Skin www.pcaskin.com

Drunk Elephant www.drunkelephant.com

NeoCutis www.neocutis.com

Jan Marini www.janmarini.com

Hylunia www.hylunia.com

Ilike buyilike.com

OSEA www.oseamalibu.com

One Ocean www.oneoceanbeauty.com

Pevonia pevonia.com

Bio Elements www.bioelements.com

Skin Script www.skinscript.com

Insurance Providers:

ISPA association, Hands on Trade insurance, Esthetician Alliance. You may even get yours through the salon you are affiliated with but know that the insurance *won't follow you if you leave.*

BUSINESS PLAN

"The business plan is your roadmap to success,

as your spa manual is your atlas." Jesseca M Smith

- <u>Monthly Lease/</u>
  <u>Mortgage Payment.</u> Depending on the size of space you intend on using, you need to consider how many services you will have to perform in order to cover the day-to-day costs to run the basic operations. If ran efficiently, the number of services performed and money brought in should far exceed the expenses and this is what should support your rent/lease or mortgage payment for your space, equipment cost or leases, and also support you with a pretty decent income.

- <u>Cost of Goods to Sell for Retail.</u> Your retail sales, or as I like to call it your "front end" should fully support the overhead it takes to run your phones, front desk help, laundry, and anything that helps support, promote and help the spa run more efficiently. Choose your retail to support the services you provide. Every guest should go home with products that support the service they received and the skincare regimen they can comfortably maintain. Be sure to check your local laws to find out if you need a re-sellers permit.

✳ Note- you may choose to start with used equipment. Find on Facebook Marketplace, LetGo or OfferUP. I've found great deals on Facial equipment gently used for my school from estheticians who were looking to upgrade or simply get out of the business.

• <u>Cost to Renovate Your Business to Meet State Code.</u> Be sure to check your state codes, laws, rules and regulations. If you choose to run your business as a mobile unit or even out of your home, you **must** be sure you are meeting all state laws, rules and regulations or your license can and will be revoked; you can be fined, or worse, jail. Some neighborhoods don't allow small businesses in homes because of covenants or HOA's. Most inner cities have zoning laws where certain businesses are allowed in those areas only. *Be sure to check with your city planners before making a big investment.* I personally ran into an issue back in the late 90's when my first spa, the Avocado Tree, was inspected by the fire department. Not only did I not have a fire extinguisher on premises, I also installed treatment room doors that were too narrow! After having to shut down and get reinspected, this was a costly and avoidable mistake!

Jesseca and her husband building a wall for one of her spa rooms

<u>Property and Liability Insurance.</u> Most aggregate and property insurance can be acquired through local and national associations. I have many listed on the vendors and suppliers page.

<u>Business License Cost.</u> Some states require state, city, and operator's licenses. Be sure you know all the licensing requirements before you open your doors and that you have the required licenses all on your wall.

<u>Cost of Beauty Supplies and Esthetician Tools.</u> Depending on the type of spa you want to open will determine the cost of your supplies and tools. You may want to take out an SBA loan. They are very low interest and have high approval odds to minority (women) business owners.

<u>Cost of Basic Materials,</u> Tables, chairs, mirrors, and waiting area furniture. This is the fun part. To design the look and feel of your space. Large or small, **it's all in the details.** Start tucking your special pieces away for the day you'll open. Yard sales, estate sales, grandma's house, you name it. Shop for those unique pieces that'll get your audience talking and to remember you.

<u>Don't Forget to Set the Tone with Good Music and Sound.</u> Get a good sound system and music. My favorite's are: Peter Kater, European Spa, ASTRON, Sayama, Celtic Serenity, Bunraku, David Arkenstone, Massage Tribe, Ebb & Flod, Patrick Bernard, i-Reiki, Akiko Usui, ParajatTerry Oldfield, Eric Chapelle, Franchesca Farini to name a few.

60

- <u>Business Expenses,</u> a computer, webpage, telephone, business cards, cable TV subscription, and magazine subscriptions are a great start. I've personally found that all of this doesn't have to really cost much. Vistaprint has really done a lot these days to lower these costs for instance; $18 website, or 500 business cards for $50 and they have sales all the time. GoDaddy, WIX, Square web hosting have great deals as well. Zazzle and Moo Cards are also good choices.

- <u>Scheduling Software</u> can cost thousands like Envision, or $20 a month. Schedulista is a Seattle company, and charges $20 for one provider and $40 for multiple as a scheduling system (2019 prices). Orchid or Boulevard is a business that provides everything for the Medi-Spa set up. Gloss Genius is great for a single room proprietor. Swipe Simple & Clover, MangoMint or MindBody have lower rates when you average more than $1.000 weekly. Square can manage your POS (point of sale), clients and can be your scheduling system at a higher percentage. There are many out there. Back in the 90's and early 2000 I had to rent a machine for 3 years minimum that processed credit cards and pay a separate fee to the bank and each credit card company! These days things have become simplified and streamlined.

- <u>Advertising and Marketing Campaigns</u>. Facebook, Instagram, Google, Pinterest and Yelp are some examples. Although these are usually free, they may ask you to "advertise" to be moved up in ratings.

- Your own Costs for Your Basic Living Needs: Rent/mortgage, transportation, food, medical insurance are all a good start to figure out your cost of living expenses. Don't forget to pay yourself; in fact, **always pay yourself**. Find value in all that you do and your guests will find value in **you**.

- Accountant. **I highly recommend finding an accountant**. For example; you will need to file B&O taxes if in Washington State, possible if doing business in other states too. Be sure you are setting aside your tax money collected for quarterly taxes. Your accountant will set you up for all of this in the beginning.

- Extra Expenses for Repairs and Other Unexpected Costs. It's a good idea to have two separate accounts. One for taxes. One for unexpected repairs or expenses. Have your accountant help you set moneys aside every week or month in each account accordingly. You will thank yourself!

- One last thing… Costs to continue your education!! Many product lines give education at a discounted rate for loyalty. Consider OTI (Oncology Training International. They give discounts to those who are Sensitive Skin Specialists and trained with the Hale and Hush skin care line.

The breakdown: Average start up cost for stand alone single room $20-$30,000. Average start up cost for multi-room Day or Medi-Spa $85-$150,000 depending on types of equipment. Adding lasers and such can easily accumulate to $250,000 and up.

Well appointed Esthetics Suite

Note: It takes time to grow a good business. Generally count on about three years until you have a steady-thriving practice. Patience is a virtue in this trade but your services will speak for themselves. Work hard but take care of yourself. Use proper ergonomics and stretch. The clients/patients will come.

<u>Sample Medi-Spa Menu</u>

Facial $85-150

Spa Facial $95-200

Mini Facial $35-65

Teen/Acne Facial $55-110

Microdermabrasion $55-150

LED $55-150

Micro-current $110-150

Micro-needling $400-$1000 for a series

ULTHERAPY $200+

Body Wrap $110+

Back Treatment $110

Ultrasonic $110-150

Facial Peel Light Depth/Medium Depth $95-300 Injectables:

Restalyne/Botox/Dysport/Hyaluronic price per unit varies

Fraxel or other Laser price per area varies

Waxing (full face and/or body) price per area varies

Brow & Lash Tint $15-45

Lash Lift (perm) $85+

Eyelash Extensions $150-300

Manicure Station $35-85

Pedicure Station $55-100

Hair Station $45-300

VI Peel or other price varies

Additional Advanced Machines vary example: HydraFacial ™

and JetPeel ™

Note: Be sure to structure your menu and pricing to match the pricing in your area. If you are setting up in a place that doesn't offer these services, then check your surrounding area to be sure your services aren't overpriced.

Groupon and Living Social are great platforms to get your name out there but I don't recommended running these promotions full-time. In the long run, they could lessen the value of your services and the services offered everywhere. But, I have used them to get my name out there. As I recruited new business, I offered incentives to keep them coming back after the initial deal. Some have become my most loyal clients.

ALWAYS Continue your education!

Potential Earnings Scale.

Here is a simple formula.

# of rooms x Average cost of services x Days Open x Hours Open x Treatments Per Day = sum … now take that total, subtract 33% (average taxes) then total overhead (cost of goods including rent) this will give you a good idea of your ball park income..

Here are some real figures from my personal experience. In a one room office, working part-time meaning I'm doing 2-3 facials and some waxing per day and only 4 days a week, an esthetician can bring in around $56,000 a year.

I gave an example when I had a multi-room spa in Dallas, I could bring in around $96,000 a year and that's giving about half back to the business for supplies, taxes, overhead, etc. It was overwhelming and I had hired labor.

Now, on average, I expect to pay myself around $40 an hour and I still do okay. I teach continuing education classes which I submit to TDLR (Texas Department of Licensing and Regulation), write books and have this app (Esthetician Resource Guide APP ©) to help the new budding esthetician. These things keep me busy and bring a modest income. You aren't confined to just giving facials as an esthetician. You have many options!

Alternatively; you can find real data for your area at:

Payscale.com

Job Title	Range	Average
Spa Manager	$12k - $56k	$40,393
Spa Director	$34k - $92k	$55,573
Massage Therapist	$23k - $63k	$41,000
General / Operations Manager	$41k - $87k	$54,326
Aesthetician/ Esthetician	$15k - $35k	$29,479
Licensed Massage Therapist (LMT)	$15k - $53k	$28,000
Esthetician	$21k - $31k	$26,000

This is data found from payscale.com 2022 for the area which one of our spa's is located. payscale.com is a great resource for industry standards for Day Spa and individual practioners. Look up your payscale for your area.

Whether writing Thank You's, or sending Gift Certificates, *it's the little de-*
tails that set you apart from the rest.
Don't forget the details!

SAFETY STANDARDS

Section 5. Safety Standards

Texas Cosmetology Sanitation Laws 83.100.

Health and Safety Definitions. (New section effective March 1, 2006, 31 TexReg 1280; amended effective August 1, 2006, 31 TexReg 5952; amended effective January 1, 2008, 32 TexReg 9970; amended effective February 17, 2012, 37 TexReg 681; amended effective July 1, 2014, 39 TexReg 4650) The following words and terms, when used in this chapter, shall have the following meanings, unless the context clearly indicates otherwise. (1) Chlorine bleach solutions--A chemical used to destroy bacteria and to disinfect implements and non-porous surfaces; solution should be mixed fresh at least once per day. As used in this chapter, chlorine bleach solutions fall into three categories based on concentration and exposure time: (A) Low level disinfection (100 - 200 ppm)--Add two teaspoons household (5.25%) bleach to one gallon water. Soak 10 minutes minimum. (B) High level disinfection (1,000 ppm)--Add one-third (1/3) cup household (5.25%) bleach to one gallon water. Soak 20 minutes minimum. (C) Blood and body fluid cleanup and disinfection (5,000 ppm)--Add one and three-quarters (1 3/4) cups household (5.25%) bleach to one gallon water. Also referred to as a 10% bleach solution. (2) Clean or cleansing--Washing with liquid soap and water, detergent, anti-septics, or other adequate methods to remove all visible debris or residue. Cleansing is not disinfection. (3) Disinfect or disinfection--The use of pathogens on implements

70

chemicals to destroy pathogens on implements and other hard, non-porous surfaces to render an item safe for handling, use, and disposal. (4) Disinfectant--In this chapter, one of the following department-approved chemicals: (A) an EPA-registered bactericidal, fungicidal, and veridical disinfectant used in accordance with the manufacturer's instructions; or (B) a chlorine bleach solution used in accordance with this chapter.

(5) EPA-registered bactericidal, fungicidal, and veridical disinfectant--When used according to manufacturer's instructions, a chemical that is a low-level disinfectant used to destroy bacteria and to disinfect implements and non-porous surfaces. (6) Multiuse items--Items constructed of hard materials with smooth surfaces such as metal, glass, or plastic typically for use on more than one client. The term includes but is not limited to such items as clippers, scissors, combs, nippers, tweezers, and some nails files. (7) Single-use items--Porous items made or constructed of cloth, wood, or other absorbent materials having rough surfaces usually intended for single use including but not limited to such items as tissues, orangewood sticks, cotton balls, thread, surgical tape, extension pads, some buffer blocks, and gauze. (8) Sterilize or sterilization--To eliminate all forms of bacteria or other microorganisms by use of an autoclave or dry heat sterilizer. (9) Sanitize or sanitization--To reduce the number of microorganisms to a safe level by use of an ultraviolet sanitizer.

83.101. Health and Safety Standards--Department-Approved Disinfectants. (New section effective March 1, 2006, 31 TexReg 1280; amended effective August 1, 2006, 31 TexReg 5952; amended effective July 1, 2014, 39 TexReg 4650) (a) EPA-registered bactericidal, fungicidal, and virucidal disinfectants shall be used as follows: (1) Implements and surfaces shall first be thoroughly cleaned of all visible debris prior to disinfection. EPA-registered bactericidal, fungicidal, and virucidal disinfectants become inactivated and ineffective when visibly contaminated with debris, hair, dirt and particulates. (2) Some disinfectants may be sprayed on the instruments, tools, or equipment to be disinfected. (3) Disinfectants in which implements are to be immersed shall be prepared fresh daily or more often if solution becomes diluted or soiled. (4) In all cases the disinfectant shall be used in accordance with the manufacturers' recommendation or other guidance in this rule. (5) These chemicals are harsh and may affect the long term use of scissors and other sharp objects. Therefore, the department recommends leaving items in solution in accordance with the manufacturers' recommendation for effective disinfection. (b) Chlorine bleach solutions shall be used as follows: (1) Chlorine bleach at the appropriate concentration is an effective disinfectant for all purposes in a salon. (2) Chlorine bleach solutions shall be mixed daily. (3) Chlorine bleach shall be kept in a closed covered container and not exposed to sunlight. (4) Chlorine bleach may affect the long-term use of scissors and other sharp objects so the department does not recommend leaving items in bleach solution beyond 2 minutes for effective disinfection (5 minutes if disinfecting for blood contamination). (5) Chlorine bleach vapors might react with vapors from other chemicals. Therefore chlorine bleach shall not be placed or stored near other chemicals used in salons (i.e. acrylic monomers, alcohol, or other disinfecting products) or near flame.

72

(6) Used or soiled chlorine bleach solution shall be properly disposed of each day. 83.102. Health and Safety Standards--General Requirements. (New section effective March 1, 2006, 31 TexReg 1280; amended effective August 1, 2006, 31 TexReg 5952; amended effective February 17, 2012, 37 TexReg 681) (a) All cosmetology establishments and licensees shall utilize clean and disinfected equipment, tools, implements, and supplies in accordance with this chapter, and shall employ good hygiene habits while providing cosmetology services. (b) A licensee may not perform services on a client if the licensee has reason to believe the client has a contagious condition such as head lice, nits, ringworm, conjunctivitis; or inflamed, infected, broken, raised or swollen skin or nail tissue; or an open wound or sore in the area to be serviced. (c) Multi-use equipment, implements, tools or materials not addressed in this chapter shall be cleaned and disinfected before use on each client. Except as otherwise provided in this chapter, chairs and dryers do not need to be disinfected prior to use for each client. (d) Single-use equipment, implements, tools or porous items not addressed in this rule shall be discarded after use on a single client. (e) Electrical equipment that cannot be immersed in liquid shall be wiped clean and disinfected prior to each use on a client. (f) All clean and disinfected implements and materials when not in use shall be stored in a clean, dry, debris-free environment including but not limited to drawers, cases, tool belts, rolling trays, or hung from hooks. They must be stored separate from soiled implements and

materials. Ultraviolet electrical sanitizers are permissible for use as a dry storage container. Noncosmetology related supplies must be stored in separate drawers or locations. (g) Shampoo bowls, and manicure tables shall be disinfected prior to use for each client. (h) Floors in cosmetology establishments shall be thoroughly cleaned each day. Hair cuttings must be swept up and deposited in a closed receptacle after each hair cut. (i) All trash containers must be emptied daily and kept clean by washing or using plastic liners. (j) Hand washing facilities, including hot and cold running water must be provided for employees. (k) Clean towels shall be used on each client. Towels must be washed in hot water and chlorine bleach.

(l) Soiled towels shall be removed after use on each client and deposited in a suitable receptacle. (m) Each cosmetology establishment shall keep all products used in the conduct of their business properly labeled in compliance with OSHA requirements. (n) Hair cutting and shampoo capes shall be kept clean. A clean (one-use) cape shall be used for each client or a sanitary neck strip or towel shall be used to keep the capes from coming into direct contact with the client's neck.

83.103. Health and Safety Standards--Hair Cutting, Styling, Shaving, and Treatment Services. (New section effective March 1, 2006, 31 TexReg 1280; amended effective January 1, 2014, 38 TexReg 9520; amended effective July 1, 2014, 39 TexReg 4650) (a) Cosmetologists shall wash their hands with soap and water, or use a liquid hand sanitizer, prior to performing any services on a client. (b) All equipment, implements, tools and materials shall be properly cleaned and disinfected in-ac-

accordance with this rule prior to servicing each client. (c) After each client, the following implements shall be wiped with a clean paper or fabric towel and sprayed with either an EPA-registered bactericidal, fungicidal, and veridical disinfectant, or a high-level disinfectant chlorine bleach solution. Equipment, implements, tools and materials to be cleaned and disinfected include but are not limited to combs and picks, haircutting shears, thinning shears/texturizes, safety razors, edgers, guards and perm rods. (d) At the end of each day of use, the above items, along with any other tools, such as sectioning clips, brushes, comb and picks shall be cleaned by manually scrubbing with soap and water or adequate methods, and then disinfected by one of the following methods: (1) Complete immersion in an EPA-registered bactericidal, fungicidal, and veridical disinfectant in accordance with manufacturer's instructions; or (2) Complete immersion in a high-level disinfectant chlorine bleach solution. 83.104. Health and Safety Standards--Esthetician Services. (New section effective March 1, 2006, 31 TexReg 1280; amended effective August 1, 2006, 31 TexReg 5952; amended effective February 17, 2012, 37 TexReg 681) (a) Cosmetologists and estheticians shall wash their hands with soap and water, or use a liquid hand sanitizer, prior to performing any services on a client. Gloves shall be worn during any type of extraction. (b) Equipment, implements, tools and materials shall be properly cleaned and disinfected after servicing each client in accordance to this rule.

(c) Facial chairs and beds, including headrest for each, shall be cleaned and disinfected after providing service to each client. The chair shall be made of or covered in a material that can be disinfected. (d) After each client, multiple use implements such as metal tweezers and comedone extractors shall be cleaned and disinfected. (e) The following implements are single-use items and shall be discarded in a trash receptacle after use: cotton pads, cotton balls, gauze, wooden applicators, disposable gloves, tissues, thread, disposable wipes, lancets, fabric strips and other items used for a similar purpose as one or more of the items listed above. (f) The following items that are used during services shall be replaced with clean items for each client: disposable and terry cloth towels, hair caps, headbands, brushes, gowns, makeup brushes, spatulas that contact skin or products from multi-use containers, sponges and other items used for a similar purpose as one or more of the items listed above. (g) Items subject to possible cross contamination such as creams, cosmetics, astringents, lotions, removers, waxes, moisturizers, masks, oils and other preparations shall be used in a manner so as not to contaminate the remaining product. Applicators shall not be re-dipped in product. Permitted procedures to avoid cross contamination are: (1) Disposing of the remaining product before beginning services on each client; or (2) Using a single-use disposable implement to apply product and disposing of such implement after use; or (3) Using an applicator bottle to apply the product. 83.105. Health and Safety Standards--Temporary Hair Removal Services. (New section effective March 1, 2006, 31 TexReg 1280; amended effective February 17, 2012; 37 TexReg 681) (a) Cosmetologists and estheticians shall wash their hands with soap and water, or use a liquid hand sanitizer, prior to performing any services on a client. (b) Cosmetologists and estheticians shall clean the areas of the client's body on which the service is to be administered.

(c) Cosmetologists and estheticians performing temporary hair removal services involving the use of depilatories, preparations or tweezing techniques shall dispose of after each use all products or single use items that have been in contact with a client's skin. (d) All wax pots shall be cleaned and disinfected in accordance with manufacturer's recommendations. No applicators shall be left standing in the wax at any time and wax may not be reused under any circumstances. (e) Thread shall be stored in a sealed bag or covered container until ready to use and shall be kept in a clean, dry, debris-free storage area. (f) All multi-use items shall be properly cleaned, disinfected and sterilized or sanitized prior to each service, in accordance with this chapter. 83.106. (washable materials) shall be cleaned by manually brushing or other adequate methods to remove all visible debris after each use, and then sprayed with an EPA-registered bactericidal, fungicidal, and veridical disinfectant, or a or a high level chlorine bleach solution in accordance with this chapter. 83.111. Health and Safety Standards--Blood and Body Fluids. (New section effective March 1, 2006, 31 TexReg 1280) (a) Blood can carry many pathogens. For this reason licensees should never touch a client's open sore or wound. Powdered alum, styptic powder, or a cyanoacrylate (e.g. liquid-type bandage) may be used to contract the skin to stop minor bleeding, and should be applied to the open area with a disposable cotton-tipped instrument that is immediately discarded after application. (b) In the case of blood or body fluid contact on any surface area such as a table, chair, or the floor, an EPA-registered hospital grade disinfectant, a tuberculocidal disinfectant, or a 10% bleach solution (one-and-three quarters (1 ¾) cups of household (5.25%) bleach to one gallon of water) shall be used per manufacturer's instructions immediately to clean up all visible blood or body fluids. (c) If any non-porous instrument is contacted with blood or body fluid, it shall be immediately cleaned and disinfected using an EPA-registered hospital grade disinfectant, a tuberculocidal disinfectant in accordance with the manu-

manufacturer's instructions, or totally immersed in a 10% bleach solution (one-and-three quarters (1 ¾) cups of household (5.25%) bleach to one gallon of water) for 5 minutes. (d) If any porous instrument contacts blood or body fluid, it shall be immediately double-bagged and discarded in a closed trash container or biohazard box.

83.112. Health and Safety Standards--Prohibited Products or Practices. (New section effective March 1, 2006, 31 TexReg 1280; amended effective February 17, 2012, 37 TexReg 681) (a) Licensees may not use any of the following substances or products in performing cosmetology services: (1) Methyl Methacrylate Liquid Monomers, a.k.a., MMA. (2) Razor-type callus shavers designed and intended to cut growths of skin such as corns and calluses, e.g., credo blades. (3) Alum or other astringents in stick or lump form. (Alum or other astringents in powder or liquid form are acceptable.) (4) Fumigants such as formalin (formaldehyde) tablets or liquids. (b) Possession on licensed premises of any item listed in this section is a violation under this chapter. (c) The use of any product, preparation or procedure that comes into contact with or penetrates the dermis layer of the skin is prohibited.

83.113. Health and Safety Standards--FDA. (New section effective March 1, 2006, 31 TexReg 1280) (a) Licensees shall not use any product in providing a service authorized under the Act that is banned or deemed to be poisonous or unsafe by the United States Food and Drug Administration (FDA) or other local, state, or federal governmental agencies responsible for making such determinations. (b) Possession or storage on licensed premises of any item banned or deemed to be poisonous or unsafe by the FDA or other governmental agency shall be considered prima facie evidence of its use. (c) For the purpose of performing services authorized under the Act, no licensee shall buy, sell, use, or apply to any person liquid monomeric methyl methacrylate (MMA).

(New section effective March 1, 2006, 31 TexReg 1280;

amended effective August 1, 2006, 31 TexReg 5952 amended effective October 11, 2007, 32 TexReg 7050; amended effective January 1, 2016, 40 TexReg 8759) (a) Establishments shall keep the floors, walls, ceilings, shelves, furniture, furnishings, and fixtures clean and in good repair. Any cracks, holes, or other similar disrepair not readily accessible for cleaning shall be repaired or filled in to create a smooth, washable surface. (b) All floors in areas where services under the Act are performed, including restrooms and areas where chemicals are mixed or where water may splash, must be of a material which is not porous or absorbent and is easily washable, except that anti-slip applications or plastic floor coverings may be used for safety reasons. Carpet is permitted in all other areas. (c) Plumbing fixtures, including toilets and wash basins, shall be kept clean. They must be free from cracks and similar disrepair that cannot be readily accessible for cleaning. (d) Each establishment must have suitable plumbing that provides an adequate and readily available supply of hot and cold running water at all times and that is connected for drainage of sewage and potable water within the areas where work is performed and supplies dispensed. (e) Every establishment shall provide at least one restroom located on or near the premises of the establishment. For public safety, chemical supplies shall not be stored in the restroom. (f) Food or beverages shall not be prepared on licensed premises for sale. Pre-packaged food or beverages may be sold to or consumed by clients. (g) For public health and safety, licensed premises shall eliminate any strong odors through adequate ventilation, including but not limited to, exhaust fans and air filtration to exhaust chemicals and fumes away from the public area and to provide for the input of fresh air. (h) Licensed premises shall not be utilized for living or sleeping purposes, or any other purpose that would tend to make the premises unsanitary, unsafe, or endanger the health and safety of the public.

An establishment that is attached to a residence must have an entrance that is separate and distinct from the residential entrance. Any door between a residence and a licensed facility must be closed during business hours. (i) Only service animals are allowed in establishments. Covered aquariums are allowed provided that they are maintained in a sanitary condition. 83.115. Health and Safety Standards--Eyelash Extension Application Services. (New section effective February 17, 2012, 37 TexReg 681)

(a) A licensee offering the eyelash extension application service shall wash his or her hands with soap and water prior to performing any services on a client. (b) Equipment, implements, and materials shall be properly cleaned and disinfected prior to providing services. (c) Chairs and beds, including headrests, shall be cleaned and disinfected after providing services to each client. The chair and beds shall be made of or covered in a nonporous material that can be disinfected. (d) After each client, the following implements shall be cleaned and disinfected: tweezers, nasal aspirator or electric eyelash dryer and other items used for a similar purpose. (e) The following implements are single-use items and shall be discarded in a trash receptacle after use: disposable gloves, tissues, disposable wipes, fabric strips, surgical tape, eye pads, extensions, cotton swabs, face mask, brushes, extension pads and other items used for a similar purpose. (f) The following items that are used during services shall be replaced with clean items for each client: disposable and terry cloth towels, hair caps, headbands, brushes, gowns,

80

spatulas that contact skin or products from multi-use containers. (g) A licensee shall use only properly labeled semi-permanent glue and semi-permanent glue remover that must be used according to the manufacturer's instructions. (h) Extensions must be stored in a sealed bag or covered container and shall be kept in a clean dry, debris-free storage area.

Section 1602.406. Infectious and Contagious Diseases (a) A person holding an operator license, instructor license, or specialty certificate may not perform any practice of cosmetology if the person knows the person is suffering from an infectious or contagious disease for which the person is not entitled to protection under the federal Americans with Disabilities Act of 1990 (42 U.S.C. Section 12101 et seq.). (b) A person holding a beauty shop license, specialty shop license, private beauty cul-

ture school license, or license to operate a vocational cosmetology program in a public school may not employ a person to perform any practice of cosmetology if the license holder knows that the person is suffering from an infectious or contagious disease for which the person is not entitled to protection under the Americans with Disabilities Act of 1990. Sec. 1603.102. Sanitation Rules The commission shall establish sanitation rules to prevent the spread of an infectious or contagious disease.

81

Please follow your states laws and regulations. Remember, the law sees things in black and white. There is no grey area. If you feel you're practicing in a "grey area" and doing a service that may or may not be within your scope of practice, inquire with your states cosmetology board for guidance. It is YOUR responsibility to keep up with changing laws, rules and regulations in your industry as it is also your responsibility to continue your education and keep up with the times.

CONSIDER YOUR MORE SENSITIVE
CLIENTS, WITH CONTINUED TRAINING
WITH ONCOLOGY EDUCATION
ONCOLOGY SPA SOLUTIONS~

HIPPA COMPLIANT SPA

Section 6. HIPPA

Here are a few tips on how to be HIPPA compliant with your Medspa.

Being HIPPA compliant isn't just for the medical professional any longer. If you are gathering information of any kind, consider yourself walking a fine line for violation risks, penalties or even jail time. Be sure you and your staff are properly trained and everyone is HIPPA compliant. Guest confidentiality is the utmost importance.

Estheticians, Medical Spas, Private Practices and so on are now offering all the latest and greatest when it comes to skin care. We want our guests to come in knowing they will get the best possible treatment and procedure and most of all, tell everyone **but**, there again, is a fine line where the practice must adhere.

If you want to ensure that your practice meets all the necessary HIPAA requirements, follow these tips.

1. Be careful with confirmations. Studies show as mush as 84% of consumers now trust online reviews as much as a personal recommendation from a friend. What people say about you online matters. You may even ask your clients to provide reviews for your services. It's perfectly legal for someone to say what a great experience they had. They can even mention staff members by name and provide whatever details they'd like.

However; when you, your staff, or named business go online and confirm their statements, this is where things can get tricky. *You are confirming their statements.* This could be a clear HIPPA violation. Saying more than "we appreciate your kind feedback" could land you in violation territory.

You cannot disclose what your client had done or who they-worked with, even if they already have. You can thank them, but never acknowledge a relationship. When you say they are a patient or that they had "*" service provided, you are in a way revealing their private and sensitive information. Steer clear of violations and keep your responses brief.

2. Steer Clear of Advice. If someone clearly asks for advice online, do not respond. Sometimes there are open forums where there can be question and answer blogs or feedback, be sure to refrain from specifics-it's a very slippery slope that could land you in court.

If someone on a forum is a current client and you accidentally reveal that status, you've violated their privacy. If a discussion turns to specifics, turn back. Your best bet might be to avoid responding at all and to answer questions with links to your-blog or service pages.

For LinkedIn, Instagram, Facebook, etc, it's best to **turn off** the commenting section in my opinion.

Another example is someone who suspects they might have an issue could end up following a thread not intended for them. If you think someone needs your advice, refer them to schedule an appointment so you can give that feedback privately.

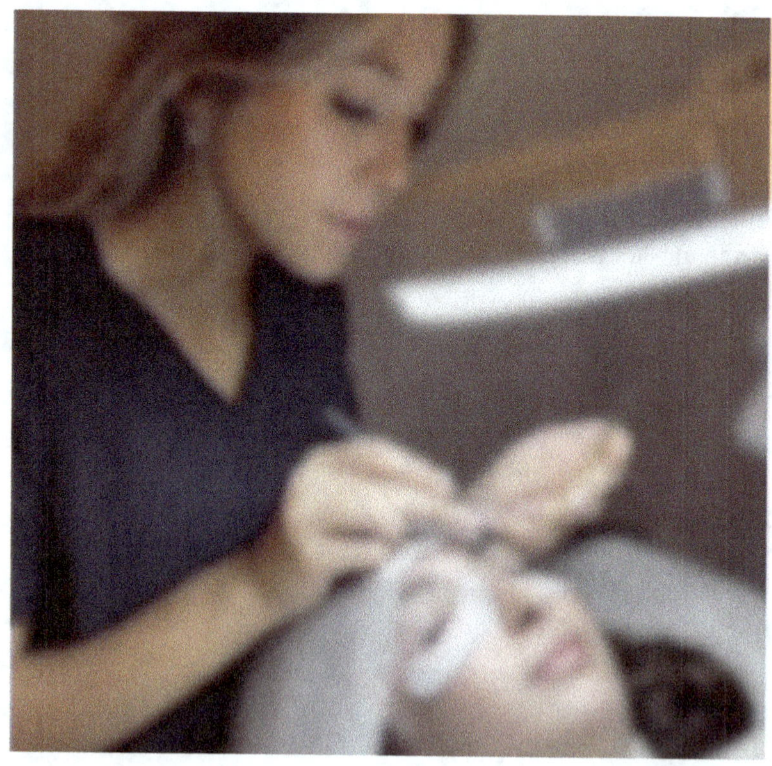

3. Disclaimers! Add disclaimers to your social media profile and any forum that you post to (never work outside your scope of practice).

Are you a blogger? If so, include a disclaimer that allows people to know that you're not giving out medical advice. Don't give out medical advice.

The internet is a public venue where everyone has access to everything. If patients/clients are posting comments, they should know that they could be posting private information to a public group of people. This is where your disclaimer will come in handy; otherwise you may have to worry about having any HIPPA investigators coming around.

4. Photos Can Cause Problems. Make sure you don't include any patients or clients in the photos you take and post on social media or in your marketing materials. If you imply that anyone but your staff or hired actors are patients at your practice, you could be violating HIPAA requirements for privacy.

If you take any photos of patients/clients, make sure you have signed permission before you publish anything. Just because you block out faces or only show a part of their body doesn't guarantee their anonymity. Show respect for your clients and get them to sign a waiver.

5. Dispose of Waste/Trash Properly. If you have any personal information that goes in the trash, make sure that you secure your trash cans and that they're picked up from a trusted disposal company. You can find a trusted disposal company online in your city. Some hospitals have shredding services or set aside a shredder for any patient information.

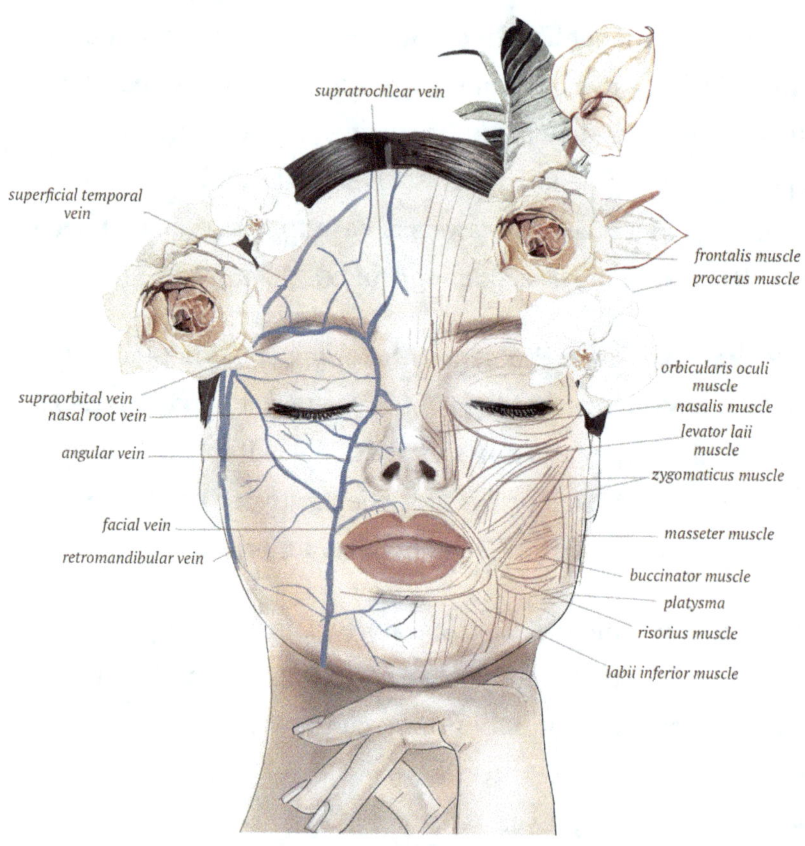

FIND FACIAL VEIN ART ON ETSY STORE ENORASIS

Identity theft can happen just through poorly disposed of trash.
Even writing information on a notepad or sticky note could reveal
sensitive information. Shred it, block it out, dispose of it properly.
Pick up a HIPAA compliant shredder (available at amazon.com) and
use it religiously. Train staff to get into the habit of using it too.

6. Keep Conversations Private. Casual conversations are unprofessional and could give away more than you may realize.
If someone sees another patient walking in and then hears details,
they could be privy to information that is meant to be private. Don't
mention anything at the front desk. It's disrespectful to your patients
and shows a lack of professionalism let alone a disregard for
HIPAA requirements.

Charts shouldn't be left out in visible areas. If there is information,
it should be hidden in an envelope, not marked with the name of the
patient they pertain to.

Sometimes we must discuss our clients or patients. Figuring out
anomalies, skin disorders, etc., but if you're having conversations
about any of your patient's details, make sure they're happening in
the privacy of your office. Casual conversations are unprofessional
and could give away more than you realize.

If someone sees another patient walking in and then hears details, they could be privy to information that is meant to be private. Don't mention anything at the front desk. It's disrespectful to your patients and shows a lack of professionalism with a disregard for HIPAA requirements.

Charts should not be left out in visible areas. If there is information, it should be hidden in an envelope, not marked with the name of the patient it pertains to.

7. Patient Lists Should Be Private. If you've got lists of your patients, people who are selling services or marketing for pharmaceutical companies might want that information. Selling patient information is illegal. Recklessly allowing someone to get ahold of it has its consequences as well.

Learning how to be HIPAA compliant takes time It could take some trial and error to get your office to become completely HIPAA compliant. Although you may want to respond immediately on social media, or if you live in a small town and mention who you saw the other day. . . don't do it! Keep quiet. Let your guests do the talking.

Let your guests take those pictures outside your spa, but refrain from commenting yourself.

INGREDIENTS

AT OUR FLAGSHIP STORE, MISSION DAY SPA, WE PROVIDE
TINTED SUNSCREEN THAT IS CRUELTY FREE, NON COMEDOGENIC
AND REEF FRIENDLY

Basic Cosmetic Ingredients Every Esthetician Should Know

Hyaluronic Acid As the chief glycosaminoglycan in **skin**,
hyaluronic acid works to keep every aspect of **skin** stable,
safeguarded, and constantly
renewed. **Hyaluronic acid** is also a humectant, which is a

93

category of-skin **care ingredients** that are hygroscopic, **meaning** they draw moisture from their surroundings. Skin care products containing this substance are often used with vitamin C products to assist in effective penetration. Hyaluronic acid (also known as a glycosaminoglycan) is often touted for its ability to "reverse" or stop aging. In news reports, you might have heard of hyaluronic acid as the "key to the fountain of youth." This is because the substance occurs naturally (and quite abundantly) in humans and animals, and is found in young skin, other tissues, and joint fluid. Hyaluronic acid is a component of the body's connective tissues, and is known to cushion and lubricate. As you age, however, the forces of nature destroy hyaluronic acid. Diet and smoking can also affect your body's level of hyaluronic acid over time. Skin care products with hyaluronic acid are most frequently used to treat wrinkled skin.

Urea Natural moisturizing **ingredient** that retains moisture and softens **skin**. **Urea** is made when proteins are broken down in the body, and so it is a natural moisturizing factor that is already present in the **skin**.

Mineral Oil Mineral oil is a clear odorless liquid that has been used routinely for many decades in a wide variety of cosmetics and personal care products. The mineral oil used in cosmetics and personal care products (also called "white mineral oil") is a highly purified material obtained from refining petroleum. It is refined to meet specifications appropriate for its use in pharmaceuticals, foods and cosmetics and personal care products.

Petroleum Jelly Petroleum jelly (also called petrolatum) is a mixture of mineral oils and waxes, which form a semisolid jelly-like substance. This product hasn't changed much since Robert Augustus Chesebrough discovered it in 1859. Chesebrough noticed that oil workers would use a gooey jelly to heal their wounds and burns. He eventually packaged this jelly as Vaseline. Petroleum jelly's benefits come from its main ingredient petroleum, which helps seal your skin with a water-protective barrier. This helps your skin heal and retain moisture. Also found in VASELINE!

Rose Water Or Rose Syrup is the hydrosol (or by-product) portion of the distillate of rose petals, generated in a process used for the production of rose oil for perfumes.Rose Water is used to flavor food, as a component in
some cosmetic and medical preparations, and for religious purposes throughout Europe and Asia.

Aqua/Water Is used in the formulation of virtually every type of **cosmetic** and personal-care product. ... Water is primarily used as a solvent in cosmetics and personal **care products** the **ingredients** that impart **skin benefits**, such as conditioning agents and cleansing agents.

Kaolin Naturally occurring clay mineral (silicate of aluminum) used in cosmetics for its absorbent properties. **Kaolin's** absorbent properties make it a popular **ingredient** in clay masks for oily **skin**. Used too often in high amounts, it can be drying, but is otherwise a benign **ingredient**.

Caprylic/Capric Triglycerides A mixed triester derived from coconut oil and glycerin. ... **Caprylic**mainly works as an emollient, dispersing agent and solvent. As an emollient, it both quickly penetrates the surface to condition the **skin/** hair, and provides a lightweight and non-greasy barrier of lubrication.

Acetyl Glucosamine Amino acid sugar and primary **constituent** of mucopolysaccharides and hyaluronic acid. **Acetyl Glucosamine** is a **skin-** replenishing **ingredient** that can have considerable value in **cosmetic products** aimed at diminishing signs of aging.

Xanthan Gum. Natural ingredient used as a thickening agent, texture enhancer, and to stabilize emulsions, which is a general term for mixtures of unlike substances such as oil and water.

Guar Gum Cyamopsis Tetragonoloba (**Guar**) **Gum** (also called **Guar Gum**) is a resinous material made from the **guar** bean. ... **Guar Gum** and the other **guar** derivatives

guar bean. ... Guar Gum and the other guar derivatives may also be used in bath products, hair care products, shaving preparations and skin care products.

Phenoxyethanol is a preservative used in many cosmetics and personal care products. You may have a cabinet full of products containing this ingredient in your home, whether you know it or not. Chemically, phenoxyethanol is known as a glycol ether, or in other words, a solvent

Methylparaben Is an anti-fungal and preservative that is widely used in cosmetics. Because it is easily absorbed through the skin and is generally considered non-irritating, it is a very popular beauty product ingredient (Wikipedia) and is used to prevent fungal growth and to generally preserve formulas

Citric Acid (AHA) Anti-Fungals a member of the alpha hydroxy family of molecules that are derived from the use of the acids in lemons, limes, oranges, and grapefruits. ... Citric Acid exfoliates the complexion, which results in ridding of dead skin.

Propylene Glycol. Along with other glycols and glycerol, propylene glycol is a humectant (hydrating) and delivery ingredient used in cosmetics. ... In cosmetics, propylene glycol is used in small amounts to keep **products** from melting in high heat or from freezing. It also helps active **ingredients** penetrate **skin**.

Glycerin Also called **glycerol** or **glycerine**, **glycerin** is a humectant that's present in all natural lipids (fats), whether animal or
vegetable. ... **Glycerin** is a **skin**-replenishing and **skin**- restoring **ingredient**, **meaning** it is a substance found naturally in **skin**, helping to establish normal balance and hydration. **Lanolin** (from Latin lāna 'wool', and oleum 'oil'), also called wool wax or wool grease, is a wax secreted by the sebaceous glands of wool-bearing animals. ...**Lanolin** and its derivatives are used in the protection, **treatment** and beautification of human **skin**.

Linoic Acid Naturally occurring, colorless polyunsaturated fatty **acid** liquid that functions as a **skin**-conditioning agent and **skin**- restorative **ingredient**. Also known as **alpha-linolenic acid**,
this **ingredient** is a plant-based omega-3 fatty **acid** that occurs in vegetable oil and flax seed oil as well as canola and soy oils. Used as an emulsifier.

Stearic Acid Is a fatty **acid** found primarily in animal derivatives, but in vegetable fats as well. It is used in a variety of cosmetics and personal **care products**, as a fragrance **ingredi-ent**, surfactant and emulsifier.

Tocopherol, or **vitamin E** a fat-soluble vitamin is a naturally occurring antioxidant which can be isolated from vegetable oil. ... Potassium Ascorbyl **Tocopheryl Grape-seed**Phosphate, a salt of both **vitamin E (Tocopherol)** and vitamin C (Ascorbic Acid) may also be used in **cosmetic products**.

Grape-seed A natural and powerful **ingredient** that works for all **skin** types, vitis vinifera isn't just about delivering nutrients to the **skin**. ... Making **grape-seed extract** perfect for those with darker **skin**, acne scarring, and sun damage. Additionally, **grape seed extract** is the perfect anti-aging **ingredient**

Papaya According to Ling Chan, founder of Ling **Skin Care** and Spa, "**Papaya** contains an enzyme called papain, which digests away dead and unhealthy **skin** cells."

Arnica Each topical contains only one active **ingredient**— **Arnica** Montana, a homeopathic medicine that has been used for centuries as a natural pain reliever. Arnicare **Cream**, Gel, Ointment, and Bruise are unscented, paraben-free, and do not contain artificial colors or perfumes. (Analgesic.)

Silk amino acid (SAAs) also known as Sericin is a natural water-soluble glycoprotein extracted from raw**silk**. It is used as an additive in **skin** and hair **care products** due to its high levels of serine which has excellent moisture preservation characteristics.

Peptides are compounds consisting of two or more linked amino acids (natural**proteins**). ... In topical **skincare** formulations, some **peptides** are shown to help provide anti-aging **benefits**.

Calendula has antiseptic properties, which are helpful for treating wounds and preventing acne. As a **skin** conditioner, **Calendula** Extract stimulates collagen production and it also reduces the occurrence of
dry **skin**. **Calendula** is a naturally occurring antioxidant

Zinc Inert earth mineral used as a thickening, lubricating, and sunscreen active **ingredient**in cosmetics. ... In the case of **zinc oxide**, nanotechnology is used to make it more aesthetically pleasing, as well as enhance its SPF. Nano-sized **zinc oxide** is
not believed to be a safety concern for **skin**.

Cucumber. Cucumis Sativus The extract of the **Cucumis Sativus** Fruit has anti-inflammatory qualities, including (sun)burns. **Cucumis Sativus** Fruit Extract can repair dry and damaged **skin**, and giving it a softer and smoother appearance.

An other benefit is that the pH-value is identical with the human-skin.

Aloe barbadensis, or **aloe vera**, is a succulent plant which offers many **benefits** and is suited for all **skin-types**, especially dry, damaged, broken, sensitive and irritated **skin**. It offers anti-inflammatory, antimicrobial, antioxidant, humectant and soothing, anti-itch qualities for **skin**.

Licorice. According to The National Cancer Institute, **Glycyrrhiza Glabra** has been used as an anti-inflammatory and antioxidant, primarily because of licochalcone, a molecule contained in **licorice** root extract which helps control oil production, and helps calm and soothe acne-prone **skin**.

Camellia New anti-aging **ingredient** extracted from leaves of **Camellia** japonica. ... **Camellia-japonica** is popular as a garden plant with beautiful flowers in Japan, and also known as a symbol of eternal beauty, therefore the extract from the leaves upgrades the cosmetics.

Green Tea What: Green tea leaf extract is produced from the leaves of the tea plant, Camelia sinensis (EWG). The extract is rich in polyphenols, free radical-fighting antioxidants, found to help prevent premature aging and guard against UV damage. The polyphenol most abundant in green tea, EGCG, is also thought by some scientists to reactivate dying skin cells.

Polysorbate 20 is used in cosmetics and **skin care products** as a surfactant, emulsifier, and fragrance **ingredient**. It is derived from Lauric Acid and is also a chemical mixture of sorbitol ethylene oxide, according to Wikipedia. It is sometimes derived from fruits and berries as well, leading to its fragrant properties.

Alpha-hydroxy acids (AHAs)

Over-the-counter skin care products containing alpha-hydroxy acids (glycolic, lactic, tartaric, and citric acids) have become increasingly popular in recent years. Creams and lotions with alpha-hydroxy acids may help with fine lines, irregular pigmentation and age spots, and may help shrink enlarged pores. Side effects of alpha-hydroxy acids include mild irritation and sun sensitivity. To avoid burning, sunscreen should be applied in the morning. To help avoid skin irritation, start with a product with a maximum concentration of 10% to 15% AHA. To allow your skin to get used to alpha-hydroxy acids, you should only initially apply the skin care product every other day, gradually working up to daily application.

Beta-hydroxy acid (salicylic acid)

Salicylic acid removes dead skin and can improve the texture and color-of sun-damaged skin. It penetrates oil-laden hair follicle openings and, as a result, also helps with acne. There are many skin care products available that contain salicylic acid. Some are available over-the-counter and others need a doctor's prescription. Studies have shown that salicylic acid is less irritating than skin care products containing alpha-hydroxy acids, while providing similar improvement in skin texture and color.

Hydroquinone *Phenols (Benzene Ring)

Skin care products containing hydroquinone are often called bleaching creams or lightening agents. These skin care products are used to lighten hyper-pigmentation, such as age spots and dark spots related to pregnancy or hormone therapy (melasma or chloasma). Over-the-counter skin care products such as AMBI® Fade cream contain hydroquinone. Your doctor can also prescribe a cream with a higher concentration of hydroquinone if your skin doesn't respond to over-the-counter treatments. If you are allergic to hydroquinones, you may benefit from use of products containing kojic acid instead.

Kojic Acid also is a remedy for the treatment of pigment problems and age spots. Discovered in 1989, kojic acid works similarly to hydroquinone. Kojic acid is derived from a fungus, and studies have shown that it is effective as a lightening agent, slowing production of melanin (brown pigment).

Retinol Retinol is derived from vitamin A and is found in many over-the-counter "anti-aging" skin care products. Tretinoin, which is the active ingredient in prescription Retin-A® and Renova® creams, is a stronger version of retinol. If your skin is too sensitive to use Retin-A®, over-the-counter retinol is an excellent alternative. Here's why skin responds to skin care products with retinol: cstructure that's tiny enough to get into the lower layers of skin, where it finds collagen and elastin. Retinol is proven to improve mottled pigmentation, fine lines and wrinkles, skin texture, skin tone and color, and your skin's hydration levels. Retinyl palmitate is another ingredient related to retinol, vitamin A has a molecular structure that's tiny enough to get into the lower layers of skin, where it finds collagen and elastin. Retinol is proven to improve mottled pigmentation, fine lines and wrinkles, skin texture, skin tone and color, and your skin's hydration levels. Retinyl palmitate is another ingredient related to retinol, but is less potent.

L-Ascorbic Acid This is the only form of vitamin C that you should look for in your skin care products. There are many skin care products on the market today that boast vitamin C derivatives as an ingredient (magnesium ascorbyl phosphate or ascorbyl palmitate, ascorbyl glucoside for example), but L-ascorbic acid is the only useful form of vitamin C in skin care products. With age and sun exposure, collagen synthesis in the skin decreases, leading to wrinkles. Vitamin C is the only antioxidant proven to stimulate the synthesis of collagen, minimizing fine lines, scars, and wrinkles.

Copper Peptide is often referred to as the most effective skin regeneration product, even though it's only been on the market since 1997. Here's why: Studies have shown that copper peptide promotes collagen and elastin production, acts as an antioxidant, and promotes production of glycosaminoglycans (think hyaluronic acid, as an example). Studies have also shown that copper-dependent enzymes increase the benefits of the body's natural tissue-building processes. The substance helps to firm, smooth, and soften skin, doing it in less time than most other anti-aging skin care products. Clinical studies have found that copper peptides also remove damaged collagen and elastin from the skin and scar tissue because they activate the skin's system responsible for those functions.

Alpha-Lipoic Acid You may have heard of alpha-lipoic acid as "the miracle in a jar" for its anti-aging effects. It's a newer, ultra-potent antioxidant that helps fight future skin damage and helps repair past damage. Alpha-lipoic acid has been referred to as a "universal antioxidant" because it's soluble in both water and oil, which permits its entrance to all parts of the cell. Due to this quality, it is believed that alpha-lipoic acid can provide the greatest protection against damaging free radicals when compared with other antioxidants. Alpha-lipoic acid diminishes fine lines, gives skin a healthy glow, and boosts levels of other antioxidants, such as vitamin C.

DMAE (dimethylaminoethanol)
If you've heard of fish referred to as brain food, you can thank DMAE. This substance is naturally produced in the brain, but DMAE is also present in anchovies, salmon, and sardines. DMAE boosts the production of acetylcholine, which is important for proper mental functions. DMAE in skin care products shows remarkable effects when applied topically to skin, resulting in the reduction of fine lines and wrinkles.

Squalene The saturated portion of emollient ingredient squalene, which is a natural component of human skin sebum (oil). It is a wonderfully moisturizing ingredient as well as being a source of replenishing *FATTY ACIDS* and antioxidants.

What is the difference between Squalene and Squalane? **Squalene** is a fat-soluble antioxidant that our skin produces in our sebum. It's also is found in shark liver; oil and botanical sources such as olives, rice bran, sugar cane and wheat germ. ... Around 60-85% of the oil in deep-sea sharks' livers is made up of **squalene**.

---

* *Ingredients to skip if you are pregnant or breastfeeding*

- Aluminum chloride hexahydrate: Found in antiperspirant; check for aluminum chloride hexahydrate and aluminum chlorohydrate.

- Beta hydroxy acids: Salicylic acid, 3-hydroxypropionic acid, trethocanic acid and tropic acid.

- Chemical sunscreens: Avobenzone, homosalate, octisalate, octocrylene, oxybenzone, oxtinoxate, menthyl anthranilate

and oxtocrylene.

- Diethanolamine (DEA): Found in hair and body products; stay clear of diethanolamine, oleamide DEA, lauramide DEA and cocamide DEA.
  Dihydroxyacetone (DHA): Found in spray self-tanners; could be harmful if inhaled. (Be sure the room is well ventilated if you choose to spray)

- Formaldehyde: Found in hair straightening treatments, nail polishes and eyelash glue; look for formaldehyde, quaternium-15, dimethyl-dimethyl (DMDM), hydantoin, imidazolidinyl urea, diazolidinyl urea, sodium hydroxymethylglycinate, and 2-bromo-2- nitropropane-1,3-diol (bromopol).

- Hydroquinone: A lightening agent; abstain from hydroquinone, idrochinone and quinol/1-4 dihydroxy benzene/1-4 hydroxy benzene.
  Parabens: Keep away from propyl, butyl, isopropyl, isobutyl and methyl parabens.

- Phthalates: Found in products with synthetic fragrances and nail polishes; avoid diethyl and dibutyl especially.
  Retinol: Vitamin A, retinoic acid, retinyl palmitate, retinaldehyde, adapalene, tretinoin, tazarotene and isotretinoin. (Here are some retinol alternatives.)

- Thioglycolic acid: Found in chemical hair removers; can also be labeled acetyl mercaptan, mercaptoacetate, mercaptoacetic acid and thiovanic acid.
  Toluene: Found in nail polishes; skip methylbenzene, toluol and antisal 1a.

- Use herbal and home-made masks and bath powders. Pick sunscreen with zinc oxide and titanium dioxide like Sand Cloud!

- Use the makeup sparingly.

- Prefer Mineral based Make up products.

- Avoid nail polishes, whitening skin creams

- Anti-ageing creams are strict No

- Using essential oils are not harmful when used moderately

- Safe to use 2.5% – 5% of Benzoyl Peroxide for treating acne

- Avoid AHAs and BHAs (glycolic is an AHA)

- Using essential oils are not harmful when used moderately, although certain ones should be avoided all together.
  - Aniseed
  - Basil
  - Birch
  - Camphor
  - Clary Sage
  - Hyssop
  - Mugwort
  - Oak Moss
  - Parley Seed or Leaf
  - Pennyroyal
  - Peppermint
  - Rosemary
  - Rue
  - Sage
  - Tansy
  - Tarragon
  - Thuja
  - Thyme
  - Wintergreen
  - Wormwood

- Safe to use 2.5% – 5% of Benzoyl Peroxide for treating acne although check with your OBGYN and DERMATOLOGIST.

NETWORKING IDEA: HOST EVENTS AND SAMPLE CUPCAKES WITH AWARD WINNING WINE (SHOWN HERE, JACLYNN RE-NEE WINES)

Important reminders, Clients that are allergic to shellfish are generally allergic to iodine which is in algae and algaenate products. Avoid using these products at all costs.

When using natural based products, **always** refer to the client intake form for reference. Although the guest may not remember to write down what they are using or that they may be sensitive or allergic to nor think it's of importance.

Be sure to ask again before applying any mask or product for extra pre-caution. Be sure you have a cosmetics dictionary available.

Milady offers a thorough ingredient dictionary on amazon.com.

Used versions are also available. Remember, Google often offers

110

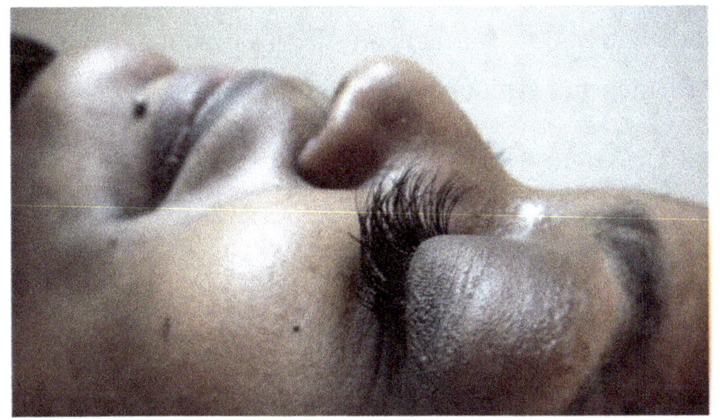

Do not cut corners with lash extensions! Take your time and get good supplies. Get your clients on a regular routine and keep them CLEAN.

NOTES & ADVICE

Section 8. Notes and advice

"We only make it, if we all do"

* Keep your sisters/fellows close. Learn who you can refer to in your trade. Keep a list of numbers in your phone of those who you trust in their work implicitly. You will call them someday, trust me!

- If you decide to do a Medical Aesthetics practice, follow HIPPA Rules and Guidelines absolutely.

- Learn your craft completely. You may not love all that your trade has to offer. i.e. eyelash extensions, if that bridal party calls your establishment, my advice is you know how to do them because I can't imagine you'll want to turn down $1,000. After, refer them to get their fills to that list of referrals you made.

- Get yourself connected to at least two good referral groups in your area. The Chamber of Commerce is a good start but there are so many more avenues these days. In Olympia, for instance, there is the *Olympia Downtown Association*, the *Thurston Talk* and the *Oly Girl Boss Collective* just to name a few. Get out, shake hands and get your wonderful face out there! Or better yet, start your own referral group!

- Start your Facebook, Instagram, Pinterest, Google and social profiles for your business but remember to **keep them professional**.

- Always continue to keep learning. Attend trade shows often.

- Give your 100% every day.

- Be on time every day.

- Be honest and never work outside your scope of practice.

- Always reach out to your mentors and seek advice.

- Remember this is a practice! You'll be practicing Esthetics for many years to come. Practice every day, keep learning.

- Stretch and have proper ergonomics.

- Bring your love of this craft to your hands every day. A gentle touch is your signature.

- Never bad talk your fellows, but give good referrals to those you trust.

- Choose brands that reflect your true passion. If it's the all natural spa you're going for, have the products you use and carry reflect that. If it's an advanced technology medical spa you're creating, choose products that reflect that vision. I've seen spas that are a combination of both whether they are medically based or holistic; just be sure you know the ingredients and believe in the brand. It will show and your passion will be contagious and draw in customers.

Notes:

____

____

____

____

____

____

How long does it take to be successful you ask?

You may be asking yourself "how long is this going to take to build my business and be self-sustaining?" My experience has proven that it depends on location and perseverance. Here are some stories about that.

Dallas, TX (2003-2006)

I worked at the time with a partner who created all natural body and facial care to combine my other passion, all things spa! We acquired a stand alone building in the popular Knox Henderson area of the city and created a storefront accompanied by a full multi-room spa in the back.

This little spa and boutique was an immediate sensation. I don't believe that city has ever had anything like that before aside from the natural market, Whole Foods! This, of course, was when the internet was still very antiquated and scarcely useful.

To get the word out, we appealed to many local papers and magazines by throwing extravagant seasonal parties that included DJ's, outdoor speakers, incentives for shoppers and spa specials.

Celebrity clients would just stroll in and shop along side our regular shoppers; the spa was booked constantly and we were doing it! It seemed like it only took a few months to really get this baby rolling.

It was **a lot** of really hard rigorous work and took up an incredible amount of energy. Soon, we found we were supporting a few locations and a manufacturing warehouse but wearing ourselves out!

In order to keep up with the clientele and in front of the media's eye, we had to constantly come up with new products, throw parties and give incentives. Eventually we took on a partnership which dissolved in 3 years; our health took a huge toll and we were just plain done. We eventually moved to Seattle and separated the two concepts and eventually sold the manufacturing portion and the company as it was, dissolved. We may have been able to keep up the momentum but it was impossible for us alone. The moral of the story? Delegate, have a plan and don't run yourself ragged even if you think you have plenty of energy to do it all yourself because it'll surely catch up with you.

Seattle, WA (2007-2014)

So I learned from Dallas and kept my practice small. Just a one-woman operation in an upstairs location in the Greenlake area. It was manageable, private and took about 4 years to get really busy. I kept my prices competitive until I was so busy that I had to raise my prices. I even hired a laundry service to help me with my workload. I attended networking groups at first and at times wondered if I'd ever be as busy as Dallas.

Eventually, word got around that my place was *the place* to go for skincare services. City Search & Yelp reviews kept pouring in. I began apprenticing new estheticians to give them experience and me a break. Later I sold the practice to one of my apprentices, which is still going strong. Slow and steady was how I grew this business. It was definitely much more manageable for me.

     Words of advice **"what are you waiting for, life is now"**.

A RECENT NEWSPAPER ADVERTISEMENT- THIS IS ACTUALLY MY MOTHER AND I! YOU CAN GET PERSONAL WITH YOUR ADVERTISING. AFTER ALL, BEING IN BUSINESS IS ALL ABOUT DEVELOPING RELATIONSHIPS. LET YOUR CLIENTS INTO YOUR PERSONAL WORLD (A LITTLE) AND SHOW THEM WHO YOU ARE OUTSIDE THE TREATMENT ROOM.

MARKETING

Section 9. Marketing

Marketing strategies ebb and flow. What I've found over the span of almost three decades is, the best marketing is word of mouth; a job well done. But, that's not to say you can't have a hand in jumpstarting your business. Granted, television and radio ads aren't as effective these days as social media ratings but how? Here are some tips that are free or close to it and you'll definitely see fruition.

- Create a Google Business Page and get your business listed on Google Maps.

- Create a Yelp, Facebook, Instagram and other pertinent business pages. . . CitySearch, WeddingWire and The Knot (the last two are marketing to the bridal industry) etc. One of the easiest ways to get listed quickly and have a higher SEO ranking is to have a business like hubspot.com or yext.com list your business for you. Often these are paid services.

- Ask your satisfied customers create 5 star ratings for you on Google, Yelp, Facebook, Wedding Wire, CitySearch and any other rating website pertinent to your area or demographic.

Business cards are you're calling cards. Have a quick link to your website like a QR code and a beautiful image that reflects the culture of your brand.

- Create a custom website with your domain and be sure it's synchronized. Usually your host will do this. Website hosts like Vistaprint has an option like "website optimize option" for approximately $10 or something like that. This automatically links your business to 100s of search engines and brings your business name up in search engine optimizers all over the web, predominantly, in your geographic area.

- Hand your business cards out like they are your only lifeline because they are.

- Put an incentive offer on your business cards; for example, $20 off your first visit or first hour visit. Also, invite your guests back with a similar offer and give them a card to give their friends and sit back and watch your business grow! Rather, get ready because you'll be busy in no time!

- Join networking groups; yes, they do work.

- Ask local marketing students at the universities to do a PR campaign on your business for credit. Now **this** does work and it's a win-win. You are helping the student and the student is helping your business. Come up with planned strategies on how you will market your business throughout the year. Have seasonal specials or offerings and feed these ideas to the students. You will surely see an increase in exposure, press and business.

- Send email campaigns through MailChimp or Constant Contact monthly. I've partnered with local real estate agents and have had my cards and full spa packages as incentives for homes sold. I've gained many clients this way. I've even been present with a table at many open houses and have met several long standing clients this way.

- Set your marketing AUTOMATIONS to be automatic on your Point of Sale platform (Square, GlossGenius, MindBody etc.) to send emails and texts to your customers for Birthdays, Welcome New Customers, Welcome them back with a Coupon … the list goes on.

- Marketing is a more think outside-of-the-box approach tool

SPONSOR A LOCAL CHEER SQUAD

- Have a stack of trusted board certified Dermatologists' cards n your office at all times and be ready to make recommendations.
- Stickers seem to be all the rage lately. Get stickers made with your logo!
- Get ALL THE MERCH with your LOGO! HATS, Robes, Private Label Cosmetics, Bags, LIP BALMS, ALL THE THINGS YOU CAN. It is your commercial!

Note: Why do Dermatologists recommend Cetaphil© so often you may ask? Dermatologists classically have loved the Cetaphil(c) cleansers because they are non-alkaline (pH 6.3-6.8), Lipid-free, non-comodegenic, and mild enough for sensitive skin. Often skin is over "sensitized" from product use or hormonal imbalance and Cetaphil© rebalances the acid mantle. Don't discount it! Re-introduce more active and professional products once the skin is more calm and rebalanced. Vanicream Gentle Facial Cleanser is also a Dermatologist favorite.*

- Have an updated copy of a cosmetics ingredients dictionary. Don't always trust Google, often it is full of opinions. Plus, you may not always have cell phone or internet access.

- Have fun every day. This is a very rewarding career!

LICENSING & ZONING

Notes:

____

____

____

____

Zoning laws, also known as zoning ordinances, define 1) what types of land use is allowed for a given area and 2) building regulations such as maximum building size or the need for fire escapes. If you're starting a business, you need to be familiar with the zoning laws that cover your building and area. Here are some of the most common municipal and federal zoning laws:

- Commercial vs residential vs manufacturing
- Type of commercial enterprise allowed, e.g. manufacturings restaurant, retail or medical
- Health and safety regulations such as use of toxic chemicals or availability of fire extinguishers
- Parking requirements
- Setback requirements
- Signage (also see City requirements)
- Types of buildings that can occupy an area (links provided)
- Size of buildings and internal requirements like multiple exits
- Floor to area ratios (FAR), e.g. you must allow for walking space, etc.
- That adequate lighting, air, and open space is provided
- Accessibility, e.g. Americans with Disabilities Act (see my example of doorway access)
-

The top 4 things you should know regarding zoning laws include:
1. What Zone Your Building Is In
2. Whether Your Business Is Allowed In This Zone
3. What Are the Building Requirements
4. What Are the Signage Requirement

Look up GIS Mapping in your area. This gives you a good idea of your location and if it's zoned for commercial.

In your laws book (if you have one) it should state whether or not you can operate as a sole provider, whether out of your home or salon and then give those parameters there as well.

Some states don't allow tattoo shops within a certain distance of a school or daycare. _This includes permanent makeup. Look into the law before opening._

<u>By state</u>

Alabama: https://aboc.alabama.gov/

Alaska: https://www.commerce.alaska.gov/web/cbpl/ProfessionalLicensing/BoardofBarbersHairdressers.aspx

Arkansas: https://www.healthy.arkansas.gov/programs-services/topics/cosmetology

Arizona: https://boc.az.gov/

California: https://www.barbercosmo.ca.gov/

Colorado: https://www.colorado.gov/pacific/dora/Barber_Cosmetology

Connecticut: https://portal.ct.gov/DPH/Public-Health-Hearing-Office/Barbers- Hairdressers-and-Cosmeticians/Examining-Board-for-Barbers- Hairdressers-and-Cosmeticians

Delaware: https://dpr.delaware.gov/boards/cosmetology/

Florida: https://www.myfloridalicense.com/intentions2.asp?chBoard=true&boardid=05&SID=

Georgia: http://sos.ga.gov/index.php/licensing/plb/16

Hawaii: https://cca.hawaii.gov/pvl/boards/barber/

Idaho: https://ibol.idaho.gov/IBOL/BoardPage.aspx?Bureau=BCB

Illinois: https://www.idfpr.com/profs/cosmo.asp

Indiana: https://www.in.gov/pla/cosmo.htm

Iowa: https://idph.iowa.gov/Licensure/Iowa-Board-of-Cosmetology-Arts-and- Sciences

Kansas: http://www.kansas.gov/kboc/

Kentucky: https://kbc.ky.gov/Pages/index.aspx

Kentucky: https://kbc.ky.gov/Pages/index.aspx

Louisiana: http://www.lsbc.louisiana.gov/ Nevada: https://sites.-google.com/nvcosmo.com/nevada-board-of-cosmetology/ home

Maine: https://www.maine.gov/pfr/professionallicensing/professions/barbers/ index.html

Maryland: https://www.dllr.state.md.us/license/cos/

Massachusetts: https://www.mass.gov/orgs/board-of-registration-of-cosmetology-and- barbering

Michigan: https://www.michigan.gov/lara/

0,4601,7-154-89334_72600_72602_72731_72864---,00.html

https://www.michigan.gov/documents/lara/ MiPLUSConverstion-FAQ2_650546_7.pdf

Minnesota: https://mn.gov/boards/cosmetology/

Mississippi: https://www.msbc.ms.gov/Pages/default.aspx

Missouri: https://www.pr.mo.gov/cosbar.asp

Montana: http://boards.bsd.dli.mt.gov/cos

Nebraska: http://dhhs.ne.gov/licensure/Pages/Cosmetology-and-Esthetics.aspx

Nevada: https://sites.google.com/nvcosmo.com/nevada-board-of-cosmetology/ home

New Hampshire:https://www.oplc.nh.gov/cosmetology/

New Jersey: https://www.njconsumeraffairs.gov/cos/Pages/default-.aspx

New Mexico: http://www.rld.state.nm.us/boards/barbers_and_cosmetologists.aspx

New York: https://www.dos.ny.gov/licensing/cosmetology/cosmetology.html

North Carolina: https://www.nccosmeticarts.com/

North Dakota: https://www.ndcosmetology.com/

Ohio: https://cos.ohio.gov/

Oklahoma: https://www.ok.gov/cosmo/

Oregon Board of Cosmetology: https://www.oregonlegislature.gov/bills_laws/ors/ors690.html

Pennsylvania: https://www.dos.pa.gov/ProfessionalLicensing/BoardsCommissions/ Cosmetology/Pages/default.aspx

Rhode Island: http://health.ri.gov/licenses/detail.php?id=225

South Carolina: https://www.llr.sc.gov/POL/Cosmetology/

South Dakota: https://dlr.sd.gov/cosmetology/default.aspx

Tennessee: https://www.tn.gov/commerce/regboards/cosmo.html

Texas: https://www.tdlr.texas.gov/cosmet/cosmet.htm

Utah: https://dopl.utah.gov/cosmo/index.html

Vermont: https://www.sec.state.vt.us/professional-regulation/list-of-professions/ barbers-cosmetologists.aspx

Virginia: http://www.dpor.virginia.gov/Boards/BarberCosmo/

Washington: https://www.dol.wa.gov/business/cosmetology/

West Virginia

Wisconsin: https://dsps.wi.gov/Pages/Professions/Cosmetologist/Default.aspx

Wyoming: http://cosmetology.wy.gov/

Peurto Rico: https://www.estado.pr.gov/en/barbers-and-barber-stylists/

District of Columbia: https://www.dcopla.com/bbc/

For any other questions or reference, please contact your local state boards.

Thank you for reading this book and I hope it was helpful in your start as a new esthetician and business owner and to avoid the pitfalls I had when starting out all those years ago. Best wishes and remember to keep your heart in it, don't let the small stuff get you down. Ask for help when you really need it and YOU CAN DO THIS! *Please feel free to reach out to me on my instagram @jessecamsmithesthetics if you have any questions. I am happy to help if I can.*

Jesseca

Create a Pinterest Page! TikTok, other~

BUILDING YOUR BRAND

Copyright vs Trademark: So, you have a business name, perhaps even a logo, a location and you want to start promoting. But have you really looked to see if there are any other businesses in the area with your brand name or logo? Are you sure? Choose carefully. Even IF you have protected your information under a trademark (™) or copyright (c) you may run into some sticky and costly red tape in the future.

So what is the Difference Between Copyright © and Trademark ™ ?While both offer intellectual property protection, they protect different types of assets. Copyright is geared toward literary and artistic works, such as books and videos.

A Trademark protects items that help define a company brand, such as its logo. Copyright protects original work, whereas a trademark protects items that distinguish or identify a particular business from another. Copyright is generated automatically upon the creation of original work, whereas a trademark is established through common use of a mark in the course of business. *To look up a patent, copyright or trademark visit this link; https://www.uspto.gov/

If you have plans of expansion; for example, you plan to take your business to other locations, cities or states, it is important to focus on brand recognition. Your brand is your culture, your vision, your baby! Protect it at all costs. I've run into this issue personally twice. Here are my stories. In the late 1990's. There were cute little solid perfumes in little tins. I got to do the artwork for them, also give input on the scents and label design. Originally, the design had a star and the perfumes were called *rockstar*. We had all the labels printed for a half a dozen scents, and as memory recalls, over 70,000 units sold for Christmas time. As they went out and shipped, we got a cease and desist letter. (This is a document sent to an individual or business to stop purportedly illegal activity and not to restart it.) The letter warned that if we didn't discontinue using the name *rockstar*, that they would take legal action and sue.

This was a very scary letter. It came from a company out of New York, who owned the rights to the label *rockstar*. Back then they had a clothing line among other things and my business, little did I know, was encroaching on thier brand name and hard work.

Long story short, we had to re-label everything. Even come up with another name. It ultimately worked out. The labels looked extra cute. We still had a star on them but renamed, *re-branded* them rather, *starlet*.

Another story, I had just moved back to my hometown Olympia, WA from Texas. I opened a small skin care business in a loft space and was ready to work. I had all my licensing and needed a name for my little spa. I had done a quick name search online and registered my business and name. I was up and running for about 6 months when I began to see promotions online for a new and similarly named skin care business in the exact same area I was working. I called the owner and found out that she was a newly graduated esthetician. She explained she searched online and decided on a name for her business, I decided changed my business name instead of making any waves since I've been here before! This time I decided my new **brand** and **name** would be Jesseca M Smith Esthetics, also JMSE Elite.

So, if you decide to open a business and have that perfect name and logo picked out and designed, check into the trade name and copyright and find out if they are registered first. This will save you a lot of heartache. Also, if you are planning to franchise or have multiple locations and expand into partnership or to sell in the future, it's imperative that these aspects are registered.

Planning for expansion: If you plan to grow, expand and possibly eventually sell, you must have a business plan. A template to follow and track your growth. Don't want to claim those hard earned tips? You better. You'll want to claim all the income you can to show your business has value. To obtain a loan for expansion, the lender may require a list the business *assets* including; net income, client lists, equipment, and longevity of the business. Tracking everything will only help you and prove value, not just *perceived value*.

Grow from one to three. I've found it was easier, when I had expanded my spa's, my business in it's entirety did far better when I went from one location to three, rather one, then two, then three. I only expanded to two locations once, and I found that the younger and less healthy business pulled from the strong established business and it was almost detrimental.

Employee vs Contractor or Renter: With growth often comes more responsibly, square footage and sometimes headache. Growth means you'll need more help. It is all up to you when deciding how to grow and structure your withholdings status.

Employees are there for specific duties outlined in your employee handbook and hire letter. They work for your company conforming to your **culture**; specific standards and protocol for a wage. Employees are often licensed professionals and must stay up to date with their licensure or you will be liable. Each state has laws for employees, tax forms and withholdings. Be sure you educate yourself. For instance, in Washington State, not only is there a minimum wage law, but also you must know the withholdings to potentially match (which include L&I and Social Security). *Contractors* can come and go as they please, set their own hours and create whatever culture they desire in exchange for a percentage compensation. *Renters* generally hold their own business shop license and often operate as their own entity unless stated in their contract. Some spas and salons require renters to dress and adhere to salon rules so the culture of the salon is consistent.

Whatever you choose, be sure to be privy of all the laws and rules regarding such. Most information is available online these days from your city and states Department of Cosmetology laws and rules section. More on Business structures pg 139-140. Difference between S.Corp, C.Corp, Sole Proprietor, LLC.

PERSONAL STORIES

Here is some advice I wanted to share with the new business owner that I have found to be helpful. The relationship you establish with your coworkers reflects the vibe and mood you set for your customers, which I believe is the most important aspect of a salon. How they feel when they walk in, and being immediately acknowledged is important, no matter whose client it is.

Your overall culture of the salon should reflect a team environment; each team player has each other's back. In essence, the salon is a family and you should look forward to going to work every day. Create a team atmosphere where you build your co-workers up instead of breaking them down by being nit picky because he/she may be messy in the break room. Instead, help them out! Also, be sure everyone participates in cleaning and assisting each other with whatever they need.

Paying attention to detail is key. For example, clean the back bar and straighten up the shelves. You will be surprised by what your guests notice.

Be sure each client has what they need when they walk out the door. Did you suggest the product that you used to make and re-create what you have just done for them? Take-home retail not only supports the look and maintenance of your guests' service but also helps your bottom line. Be sure your retail is fully stocked at all times, if possible.

As an owner and a leader, you must be firm with your standards from the get-go otherwise, things are misinterpreted. Remember what your guests see. You may have a high standard but the tone can be set by what the sloppiest person is wearing. Make sure you choose the right fit for your team!

Lastly, never rush to hire someone if you can't afford the space then have to move.

Best of luck,
Michelle Larson, Owner Olympia Hair Company

My name is Tina Cardenas. I am 47 years old. I am a licensed esthetician, licensed manicurist and have been a Registered Dental Assistant for 28 years. I was the supervising registered dental assistant for the Department of Corrections for 18 years until I medically retired. Now I teach aesthetics to amazing women at my Alma mater; CV Beauty College in La Quinta, California. I also get to fulfill my life's purpose and help women and men look their best.

I believe in energetic aesthetics; utilizing the life force energy and love and light in all I do! My favorite facial is the hydrafacial and my favorite waxing is Brazilians.
I utilize Jesseca's book when I was opening up my salon suite! I loved it so much I use it in my classroom. You will find us making masks straight out of her book!!! I am also NANA to two amazing boys and the mother of three beautiful adults.!
I would encourage someone starting out in esthetics to find a mentor. Someone who is willing to help them grow and learn. I would encourage the to keep going even when times get tough! I opened my business in February 2020! If I can succeed in a pandemic at 46 years old, anyone can succeed.

Tina Cardenas
Licensed Esthetician & Educator

As a cosmetologist my career began in 2006. I graduated high school and went straight into the first class available to me at my local cosmetology school. Once I was in, I knew that I was in the right place. I went through my fair share of struggles, and had even contemplated quitting, multiple times, but even through all of that I always felt I was doing what I was meant to do. After graduating I went to work for a local salon for a short time and then decided to move myself from my hometown in Central California, down to Southern California. I worked for Ulta & Regis while living down there, and I learned so much. I owe most of my knowledge to the wonderful manager I had when I worked for Regis, she truly went above and beyond for me. Living and working in L.A. taught me to hustle to get what I wanted, and to always keep an eye out for anything I could learn from. Once I decided to move back home, I worked for another local salon until I got the opportunity of a lifetime. I started pursuing a job at a new cosmetology school in town. After many months of interviewing and following up, the job was mine. I taught with that school for 7 years, 2 of which I was the Dean of Education. It even took me from my small hometown in California to San Antonio Texas, where I currently call home. Saying that I learned a lot from that portion of my career is an understatement. I cannot begin to quantify the number of valuable lessons I learned but I can say I am a better person in my career, and in my personal life because of it. I now manage 8 salons in 7 different cities here in Texas. I also have my own education and job placement business called Working Knowledge that I run with my wonderful wife. We have taken a simple idea and turned it into a reality. We hope to continue to grow and share it with everyone who will benefit from our combined knowledge. The reason it has been possible to do this, and have confidence that it will be successful, is due to our many years in customer service and the lives we have had leading up to deciding to pursue this dream. We took every opportunity to learn from each obstacle that came our way.My advice to all the young and or "up and coming" professionals out there, is get yourself a mentor, someone in the industry willing to share with you all that they have learned. That type of education on top of your continuing education you do already will be vital to you and your growth. Next, never stop learning, especially when you think you know it all. If you find yourself at a point in your career that you feel you know all there is to know, that is the day you should retire. We NEVER stop learning. Lastly, be patient. Building clientele and perfecting what you do takes time. Dedicate yourself to building your personal brand and learning your craft, you will build and perfect over time. -Shane Lowe

CoOwner/Lead Educator/Recruiting Specialist & Licensed Cosmetologist

I was drawn to the world of professional aesthetics back in 2004. At the time I was working a retail job at an integrative pharmacy where I found myself advising customers about holistic ways to care for and improve their skin. I was 26 years old and had recently figured out how to heal my own acne through good nutrition, balancing my hormones and the help of a talented aesthetician. Having suffered from bad skin since the age of 13, I had the deep desire to help others with their skin so I decided to take my career to the next level by becoming an aesthetician. I enrolled at the Euro Institute of Skin Care and instantly fell in love with the art and science of holistic aesthetics. I opened a private practice straight out of school and focused solely on doing what I loved: providing organic, luxurious, rejuvenating, and results-oriented European facials. My clientele quickly grew in those first couple of years and I was booked out a month in advance, my schedule filled mostly with my loyal, happy clients. I truly enjoyed going to work everyday and had an income I could depend on. I attribute my early success to one key factor: I stayed true to myself, did only what I love, and showed up for my clients with pure authenticity. Over the years my practice grew through word of mouth referrals and that continues to be my strongest source of new business to this day.

Throughout my career my clients have always said that it's clear that I love what I do. I've had several come into my treatment room, lie down on my facial bed, and say that just being there makes them want to take better care of themselves — to eat healthier, get more sleep, and to do the things that they love. This is what inspires me — that by simply doing what I love, I'm inspiring others.

So here is my advice to you: Do what you love. Do what lights you up and what inspires you to bring your best self to work everyday. Make it a special, sacred experience for your clients each and every time. Remember that they are investing their precious time and money into their self care, so it's of the utmost importance to honor that and to hold that space for them. Treat yourself with the same care that you provide your clients. Working one on one with people each day is incredibly rewarding, but it can also lead to burnout if you don't properly care for yourself. if you don't properly care for yourself. This means having healthy boundaries with your time and also with your client relationships. Be kind and compassionate, but be professional. Most of all, be yourself and don't be afraid to let your light shine brightly because ultimately what you are providing is an experience with YOU. It's your energy and your expertise that will keep them coming back.

Fauzia Morgan

Certified Nutrition Consultant and Licensed Aesthetician

My name is Jill Zimmer and I am passionate about health, wellness and living a best life. I have the privilege to be on the leadership team for Wyndmere Naturals which supports my passion for enhancing people's lives in so many ways. I feel fortunate to be a part of an established heirloom company specializing in pure essential oils and clean lifestyle products that add to mental, physical and soulful wellbeing. How did I get here? It certainly has been a circuitous path of trying to satisfy the ongoing battle of left brain and right brain, having equal division of creativity and analytical thinking. My life's path included having an art studio in Minneapolis, being a business analyst for grocery products to military bases around the world and a mixed bag of other positions. While I questioned whether or not I paved the right path many times, I knew that I would realize something that would bring it all together. So here I am, happy as a clam at Wyndmere being able to utilize my experience, passions and both brains! Phew, finally! Finding your passion and being true to it will pay off in the long run. For me the run was pretty long but thankful I am HERE!

EXTRA: Business Structures:

What Is a Corporation?

A corporation is a business entity that you form by filing incorporation documents with your state. Corporations differ from sole proprietorships, partnerships or LLCs in a variety of ways. A corporation has shareholders, directors and officers. The shareholders own stock in the company, the directors set policies and oversee the "big picture," and the officers run the company day-to-day. In a small business, one person may serve in multiple roles.

As a legal entity, a corporation is distinct from its shareholders, meaning shareholders aren't personally responsible for debts of the corporation (the shareholder liability is limited to shareholder investment). Corporations are also subject to a number of legal requirements to which other types of businesses are not. These include holding regular meetings and keeping corporate records.

138

What Is an S-Corp?

While a corporation is a type of business entity, an S-corp is a tax designation available to certain corporations and LLCs. S-corps are named from the subchapter of the Internal Revenue Code—subchapter "S"—under which the tax designation is spelled out. The most defining characteristic of an S-corp is its so-called "pass-through" tax structure.

Liability Protection

Along with the tax advantages, S-corps still enjoy the same protection from liability offered by corporation status. Similarly, S-corps maintain an independent life from an owner—meaning the departure of key shareholders isn't as big an obstacle to longevity as it might be for non-corporate business structures. This flexibility extends to relative ease in transferring ownership of the company, through either an outright or gradual sale. That said, most S-corps have some kind of transfer restriction that makes it harder for shareholders to exit than it would be for a C-corp. S-corp taxation isn't just for corporations—LLCs that meet eligibility requirements can also elect to be taxed as an S-corp. By default, LLCs are taxed like sole proprietorships or partnerships, meaning the owners are considered self-employed and pay self-employment tax on all business profits. S-corp shareholders can be company employees (rather than self-employed), reporting both a salary and distributions from company profits. S-corp shareholders only pay self-employment tax on the salary component of income, while distribution income isn't subject to self-employment taxes.

S-corps may receive extra scrutiny from the IRS, especially when it comes to the allocation of income between distribution and salary. Salaries paid to S-corp shareholders must be reasonable, and not artificially low to avoid taxes.

Alternatives To Consider

Although they have many desirable characteristics, S-corps are only one of many possible business structure designations. As always, the right choice depends on the specifics of the business. Here are some of the other most common options:

C-Corp

C-corps are the most common type of corporation—essentially the default variety—and like S-corps, the structure gets its name from the subchapter of the Internal Revenue Code under which the classification is

designated. While S-corps and C-corps are usually not any different under state corporation laws, the important differences lie in federal taxation.

With a C-corp, a corporate income tax is paid first with a federal return
(Form 1120) required by the IRS. Shareholders must then pay taxes on
personal income at the individual level for any gains from dividends.

LLC

A limited liability company balances the relative ease and flexibility of a
partnership structure with the increased risk protection and tax advantages of a corporate structure. LLC owners (known as "members") aren't
personally liable for business obligations. By default, members pay taxes
in the same way owners of a sole proprietorship or general partnership
might. But an LLC can also elect to be taxed as an S-corp or a C-corp if
it meets certain requirements. Many small business owners choose LLCs
for simplicity and flexibility and eventually elect S-corp status rather than
first registering as a corporation.

In order to establish an LLC, instead of filing Articles of Incorporation like
a corporation, LLC founders must file Articles of Organization with whatever state agency manages business registration. Just like a corporation,
an LLC must also list a registered agent.

Sole Proprietorship

If a legal distinction between business and owner—and the protections
this legal separation of entity can afford—are not important or desirable
to a business founder, a sole proprietorship could be an appropriate alternative, given other specific circumstances. Sole proprietorship is the
simplest structure for a one-owner business, giving the owner few regula-
tory burdens and a high degree of control and flexibility.

Without a distinct business entity, however, there's no legal difference
between the business's assets, debts and other liabilities and those of
the owner. Unlike a corporation, this means the owner is directly on the
hook for any legal or financial failures of the business.

Partnership

Partnerships are similar to sole proprietorships on issues of liability and
taxes. A partner of a general partnership, like a sole proprietor, reports his
or her (or its) share of income, expenses, credits, profits and losses on
personal tax returns, thus paying a personal income tax rate and assum-
ing the business's liability as personal liability.